AF182617

SpringerBriefs in Finance

For further volumes:
http://www.springer.com/series/10282

[illegible]

[illegible]

[illegible]

Guo Ying Luo

Asset Price Response to New Information

The Effects of Conservatism Bias and Representativeness Heuristic

Springer

Guo Ying Luo
DeGroote School of Business
McMaster University
Hamilton, Ontario
Canada

ISSN 2193-1720 ISSN 2193-1739 (electronic)
ISBN 978-1-4614-9368-6 ISBN 978-1-4614-9369-3 (eBook)
DOI 10.1007/978-1-4614-9369-3
Springer New York Dordrecht Heidelberg London

Library of Congress Control Number: 2013950495

Printed on acid-free paper

Springer is part of Springer Science+Business Media (www.springer.com)

Acknowledgements

I would like to acknowledge the comments and suggestions from my colleagues at McMaster University. In addition, I would like to thank the Social Sciences and Humanities Research Council of Canada (SSHRC) for the financial support.

Contents

Contents

Chapter 1
Introduction

Empirical studies in finance literature document evidence suggest the existence of the asset price underreaction and overreaction to new information. For example, Bernard and Thomas (1989) find that stock price continues to react to earnings one year after they were announced. Ikenberry et al. (1995) show a positive abnormal return four years after the open market share repurchase announcements. Ikenberry et al. (1996) study how stock price responds to the split announcements. They find a significant positive postsplit excess return in the first three years. They attribute the postsplit return to market underreaction to the positive information signaled by a split. Desai and Jain (1997) document a positive abnormal return both before and after a stock split. Also, a positive postevent abnormal return over two years after the announcement of repurchase tender offers was reported in Lakonishok and Vermaelen (1990). Michaely et al. (1995) study market reactions to initiations and omissions of the cash dividend payments and they find that the stock price underreacts to the negative information in dividend omissions and to the positive information in initiations. Jagadeesh and Titman (1993) identify the momentum effect, which is consistent with the market underreaction to new information. De Bondt and Thaler (1985) present evidence that the stocks having the lowest returns over any given five-year period tend to have high return over the subsequent five years, and vice versa. Their findings suggest that the stock price overreacting to good news by overshooting its true value must experience a correction. Some other studies document the poor long-term postevent returns of initial public offerings (see Ritter 1991; Loughran and Ritter 1995) and seasoned equity offerings (see Loughran and Ritter 1995; Spiess and Affleck-Graves 1995). The asset price underreaction and overreaction to new information are regarded as anomalies. They are not consistent with the efficient market hypothesis (Fama 1970), nor can they be explained by the rational asset pricing theory in the literature.

A few recent behavioral models presented their explanations of these phenomena. For example, Daniel et al. (1998) assume that investors suffer from self-attribution bias in interpreting their ability to pick stocks. In other words, investors attribute the good performance of winning stocks to their ability to pick stocks and the poor performance of losing stocks to bad luck. As a result, they become overconfident about their ability to pick the winning stocks and overestimate the precision of their

G. Y. Luo, *Asset Price Response to New Information*, SpringerBriefs in Finance,
DOI 10.1007/978-1-4614-9369-3_1, © The Author(s) 2014

informational signal. They push the prices of winning stocks above their fundamental values. This delayed overreaction provides an opportunity for momentum strategies to profit, which eventually is reversed as prices revert to their fundamental values.

Barberis et al. (1998) build a model based on psychological biases (namely, conservatism bias and representativeness heuristic) to generate the asset price overreaction and underreaction to new information. In their model, the asset price underreaction to new information is generated in a manner which is consistent with conservatism; and the asset price overreaction to new information is the result of representativeness heuristic. Note that the phenomenon of conservatism was identified in experiments by Edwards (1968), who analyzed a subject's reaction to new evidence relative to that of an idealized rational Bayesian. He found that an individual updated his or her posteriors in the correct direction, but not far enough relative to rational Bayesian. Representativeness heuristic is another type of psychological bias documented by psychologists in their experiments (see Grether 1980; Kahneman and Tversky 1973; Tversky and Kahneman 1974). Tversky and Kahneman (1974) state "A person who follows this heuristic evaluates the probability of an uncertain event, or a sample, by the degree to which it (i) is similar in its essential properties to the parent population, (ii) reflects the salient features of the process by which it is generated" (p. 33). Hence, when forming posterior beliefs, people with representativeness heuristic place too much weight on their current information and not enough on their prior knowledge. They underweight the base rate relative to Bayes rule. This is also referred as the base rate fallacy in psychological literature (see Grether 1980; Kahneman and Tversky 1973; Tversky and Kahneman 1974). Also, technical traders' overextrapolation of the past prices is another example of representativeness heuristic.

Hong and Stein (1999) uses the gradual diffusion of information across the population to explain the asset price underreaction to new information; and they attribute the technical traders' extrapolation based on past prices to the cause of the asset price overreaction to new information.[1] Hirshleifer et al. (2011) use investors' limited attention to different types of information to explain the causes of both under- and overreaction to different earnings components.

Frazzini (2006) uses "disposition effect" to explain the cause of asset price underreaction to news.[2] The disposition effect refers to the pattern that investors avoid realizing paper losses and seek to realize paper gains. The basic idea is as follows. When a stock experiences good news and increases in value, investors who display the disposition effect will want to sell it to lock in the paper gain. This means that the stock price will not rise as much as it would otherwise. Hence, the stock price underreacts to good news. On the other hand, when bad news is released into the market and the stock price goes down in value, disposition investors are reluctant

---

[1] Douks and McKnight (2005) and Jegadeesh and Titman (2001) empirically test and support the predictions of the behavioral models.

[2] The disposition effect is first described in Shefrin and Statman (1985). Odean (1998) and Grinblatt and Han (2005) document evidence suggesting that investors are in deed reluctant to realize capital losses and eager to sell for capital gains.

to sell, absent a premium. This prevents the stock price from falling as much as it would otherwise. Therefore, the stock price also underreacts to bad news.

In spite of different explanations for these phenomena, in literature, conservatism bias and representativeness heuristic are used to explain the cause of asset price underreaction or overreaction to new information. This book takes an interest in further examining analytically the role of conservatism bias and representativeness heuristic in causing the asset price overreaction or underreaction to new information. This book constructs different theoretical models to prove that either conservatism or representativeness is capable of generating both asset price overreaction and underreaction to new information. The results presented in this book shed some light on the cause of the asset price overreaction and underreaction to new information. However, the results are purely theoretical and they are not intended to explain the empirical phenomena.

The remainder of this book consists of six chapters. Chapter 2 examines how conservatism bias generates the asset price overreaction or underreaction to new information in a perfectly competitive securities market. In the perfectly competitive securities market, conservatism bias does not always cause the asset price to underreact to new information. With the presence of noise traders in the market, whether conservatism bias causes the asset price to overreact or underreact to new information depends on the realization of informational signal, and whether noise traders are net buyers or sellers. The occurrence of the asset price overreaction to new information can be resulted from conservatism traders taking trading positions in the same side of the market as rational traders, and at the same time, taking larger trading positions than rational traders do.

Chapter 3 proves in an alternative market structure (namely, a security market allowing for strategic interaction among traders) that conservatism bias is also capable of generating asset price overreaction or underreaction to new information.

Chapters 4 and 5 explore how the representativeness heuristic causes the asset price to overreact or underreact to new information in different market structures. Specifically, the model in Chapter 4 proves in a competitive securities market that representative heuristic causes the asset price to overreact to slightly good news or slightly bad news and underreact to extremely good news or extremely bad news. The model in Chap. 5 focuses on examining the role of representativeness heuristic in a security market with imperfect competition in causing the asset price to overreact or underreact to new information. It proves that representativeness heuristic causes the asset price to overreact to some informational signals with certain model parameter value conditions and to underreact to other informational signals with different model parameter value conditions.

Note that the models in Chap. 2–5 do not attempt to explain the empirical anomalies of asset price underreaction and overreaction to new information. Instead, it focuses on demonstrating theoretically that either conservatism bias or representativeness heuristic is capable of generating both asset price overreaction and underreaction to new information in a competitive securities market and in a security market, allowing for strategic interaction among traders.

The model in Chap. 6 attempts to explain these anomalies by using both conservatism bias and representativeness heuristic in a model of imperfect competition. The results of this model suggest that the occurrence of asset price overreaction or underreaction to new information depends on the proportion of conservatism traders, the proportion of heuristic traders, the degree of conservatism bias, the degree of representativeness heuristic, and the number of traders in the market. Specifically, the asset price overreacts to good news and underreacts to bad news if the total representativeness heuristic minus the total conservatism bias in the market is greater than zero but less than one; otherwise, the asset price underreacts to good news and overreacts to bad news. Chapter 7 presents some concluding remarks.

Chapter 2
Conservatism Bias and Asset Price Overreaction or Underreaction to New Information in a Competitive Securities Market

2.1 Introduction

This chapter proves that conservatism bias is capable of causing the asset price to overreact or underreact to good news or bad news. These results are obtained in a static equilibrium model of a competitive securities market. In the market, there are two types of assets: risk-free asset and risky asset. The payoff for the risk-free asset is one and the payoff for the risky asset is normally distributed. There are three types of traders: rational traders, conservatism traders and noise traders. Noise traders trade for liquidity reasons and hence, their demand for the risky asset is assumed to be random. Before any trade takes place, rational and conservatism traders receive an informational signal about the asset payoff. Due to the conservatism bias, conservatism traders are slow to update their beliefs about the asset payoff relative to rational traders after receiving the new information.

In this competitive securities market, the asset price overreaction to the new information occurs if in responding to the new information, rational traders buy (sell) the asset and at the same time, the asset price is higher (lower) than what it would in the market with rational traders and noise traders. In addition, the asset price underreaction to the new information occurs if rational traders buy (sell) the asset and at the same time, the asset price is not as high (low) as it would in the market with rational traders and noise traders.

For the sake of the following discussions, an informational signal is considered as good news (bad news) if the signal is greater (smaller) than the expected payoff of the asset. In addition, based on how far the signal is greater (smaller) than the expected payoff of the asset, the good news (bad news) is classified into three types of good news (bad news): slightly good news (slightly bad news), very good news (very bad news) and extremely good news (extremely bad news). Specifically, an informational signal is considered as slightly good news (slightly bad news) if the signal is very close to and bigger (smaller) than the expected payoff of the asset. On the other hand, if the signal is much larger (smaller) than the expected payoff of the asset, then the informational signal is considered as extremely good news (extremely bad news). If the signal is not very close to and also not much larger (smaller) than the expected payoff of the asset, then the signal is considered as very good news (very bad news).

G. Y. Luo, *Asset Price Response to New Information*, SpringerBriefs in Finance,
DOI 10.1007/978-1-4614-9369-3_2, © The Author(s) 2014

Due to the conservatism bias, if the signal indicates good news (bad news), a conservatism trader has a smaller (larger) conditional mean of the asset payoff than a rational trader does; and in addition, for any given signal, a conservatism trader has a larger conditional variance of the asset payoff than a rational trader does.

The following discusses how the conservatism bias causes the asset price to overreact or underreact to the good news or bad news in the case of noise traders being net sellers or buyers of the asset.

If noise traders are net sellers of the asset, then the asset price underreacts to all types of good news. The intuition behind this result is as follows. Note that in the case of noise traders being net sellers of the asset, in responding to all types of good news, rational traders view the asset as undervalued and consequently buy the asset. On the other hand, in responding to all types of good news, conservatism traders can either buy or sell the asset. If conservatism traders buy the asset, then they do not take trading positions as large as rational traders do. This is because in the case of the signal suggesting the good news, a conservatism trader has a smaller conditional mean of the asset payoff than a rational trader does; and also, a conservatism trader has a larger conditional variance of the asset payoff than a rational trader does. In addition, if conservatism traders sell the asset in responding to all types of good news, then conservatism traders take trading positions opposite to rational traders. In either case, the asset price is not as high as it would be in the market with rational traders and noise traders. That is, the asset price underreacts to all types of good news.

However, if noise traders are net buyers of the asset, then the asset price can overreact to one type of good news and underreact to the others. The intuition for these results is as follows. In the case of noise traders being net buyers of the asset, conservatism traders sell the asset in response to the slightly good news. The reason for conservatism traders selling the asset is that in the case of the signal suggesting the good news, a conservatism trader has a smaller conditional mean of the asset payoff than a rational trader does and as a result, conservatism traders view the asset as overvalued. In addition, in responding to the slightly good news, rational traders view the asset as overvalued and sell the asset. However, conservatism traders take smaller positions in selling the asset than rational traders. Consequently, the asset price is not as low as it would be in the market with rational traders and noise traders. That is, the asset price underreacts to the slightly good news. However, if the signal suggests very good news, then conservatism traders take larger positions in selling the asset than rational traders. Hence, in the case of the signal suggesting very good news, conservatism traders' aggressive selling of the asset on the same side of the market as rational traders drives the asset price lower than what it would in the market with rational traders and noise traders. That is, the asset price overreacts to the very good news.

In addition, in the case of noise traders being net buyers of the asset, if the signal suggests extremely good news, then rational traders buy the asset. The reason for rational traders buying the asset is that a rational trader has a larger conditional mean of the asset payoff than a conservatism trader does and consequently, rational traders view the asset as undervalued. However, conservatism traders sell the asset in response to the extremely good news. Hence, rational and conservatism traders take opposite trading positions, and the asset price is not as high as it would be in the market with rational traders and noise traders. Thus, the asset price underreacts to the extremely good news.

This chapter also proves that in the case of noise traders being net buyers of the asset, the asset price underreacts to all types of bad news; in addition, in the case of noise traders being net sellers of the asset, the asset price overreacts to one type of bad news and underreacts to the others. Similar intuition to the above can be applied to explaining these results.

The remainder of this chapter consists of three sections. The next section describes the model. Section 3 presents how the conservatism bias causes the asset price to overreact or underreact to the good news or bad news. The concluding remarks are in Sect. 4.

2.2 The Model

To illustrate how conservatism bias causes the asset price to overreact or underreact to good news or bad news in a competitive securities market, an extension to Grossman and Stiglitz (1980) is used. Specifically, consider a static model of a competitive securities market with one risk-free asset and one risky asset. The payoff of the risk-free asset is one and the payoff of the risky asset (denoted as θ) is normally distributed with the mean of $\overline{\theta}$ and standard deviation of σ_θ. In the market, there are three types of investors: rational traders, conservatism traders, and noise traders. Conservatism traders exhibit conservatism bias. Noise traders trade for their liquidity reasons and hence, their demand of the asset is assumed to be random[1].

Before any trade takes place, rational and conservatism traders receive an informational signal about the asset payoff. The informational signal is modeled as:

$$S = \theta + \epsilon, \tag{2.1}$$

where the residual error ϵ is normally distributed with the mean zero and standard deviation of σ_ϵ; in addition, ϵ is independent of θ. Since θ and ϵ are independently and normally distributed, rational traders update their beliefs about the mean and standard deviation of the asset payoff according to:

$$E_r\left(\theta\,|S\right) = \overline{\theta} + \frac{\sigma_\theta^2}{\sigma_\theta^2 + \sigma_\epsilon^2}\left(S - \overline{\theta}\right), \tag{2.2}$$

and

$$Var_r\left(\theta\,|S\right) = \sigma_\theta^2 - \frac{\sigma_\theta^4}{\sigma_\theta^2 + \sigma_\epsilon^2} = \frac{\sigma_\theta^2\sigma_\epsilon^2}{\sigma_\theta^2 + \sigma_\epsilon^2}, \tag{2.3}$$

respectively, where subscript r indicates a rational trader. Since θ and ϵ are independently and normally distributed, Eqs. (2.2) and (2.3) follow from the results of Theorem 1 in the appendix.

[1] Noise traders provide the liquidity to the market.

Due to the conservatism bias, conservatism traders are slow to update their beliefs about the mean and variance of the asset payoff. Hence, conservatism traders' conditional mean and variance of the asset payoff are modeled as:

$$E_c\left(\theta\,|S\right) = \overline{\theta} + m\left(E_r\left(\theta\,|S\right) - \overline{\theta}\right), \tag{2.4}$$

and

$$Var_c\left(\theta\,|S\right) = \sigma_\theta^2 + m\left(Var_r\left(\theta\,|S\right) - \sigma_\theta^2\right), \tag{2.5}$$

respectively, where subscript c indicates a conservatism trader and m is an adjustment parameter and $m \in (0, 1)$. The closer to one the adjustment parameter m, the less is the conservatism bias. If the adjustment parameter is one, then conservatism traders become indistinguishable from rational traders.

Substituting Eq. (2.2) into (2.4) results in:

$$E_c\left(\theta\,|S\right) = \overline{\theta} + \frac{m\sigma_\theta^2}{\sigma_\theta^2 + \sigma_\epsilon^2}\left(S - \overline{\theta}\right). \tag{2.6}$$

Note from Eq. (2.6) that if the signal is larger than the expected payoff of the asset, then a conservatism trader has a smaller conditional mean of the asset payoff than a rational trader does; in addition, if the signal is smaller than the expected payoff of the asset, then a conservatism trader has a larger conditional mean of the asset payoff than a rational trader does.

In addition, substituting Eq. (2.3) into (2.5) gives rise to:

$$Var_c\left(\theta\,|S\right) = \sigma_\theta^2 - \frac{m\sigma_\theta^4}{\sigma_\theta^2 + \sigma_\epsilon^2}. \tag{2.7}$$

Note from Eq. (2.7) that for any given signal, a conservatism trader has a larger conditional variance of the asset payoff than a rational trader does.

The initial wealth for each trader is assumed to be w, where $w > 0$. Since the payoff of the risk-free asset is one, it follows that there is no gain or loss from trading this asset. In the competitive market, traders take the risky asset price as given. Denote the risky asset price as p and the demand for the risky asset by trader i (where $i = r, c$) as X_i. Hence, trader $i's$ wealth (where $i = r, c$) (denoted as w_i) is the summation of his initial wealth and profit from trading the asset. That is, $w_i = w + X_i(\theta - p)$. Each trader is assumed to have an exponential utility function. That is, for trader i (where $i = r, c$), $U(w_i) = -e^{-aw_i}$, where a is the coefficient of absolute risk aversion and $a > 0$. Since the random variables θ and ϵ are independently and normally distributed, the demand function of trader i (where $i = r, c$) can be solved from:

$$\begin{aligned} &\max_{X_i} E_i(w_i\,|S) - \frac{a}{2} Var_i(w_i\,|S), \\ &s.t. \quad w_i = w + X_i(\theta - p). \end{aligned} \tag{2.8}$$

In other words, with Eqs. (2.2), (2.3), (2.6) and (2.7), optimization problem (2.8) is solved to give rise to the demand functions for rational and conservatism traders as:

$$X_r = \frac{\overline{\theta} + \eta\left(S - \overline{\theta}\right) - p}{a\sigma_\theta^2(1-\eta)}, \tag{2.9}$$

and

$$X_c = \frac{\overline{\theta} + m\eta\left(S - \overline{\theta}\right) - p}{a\sigma_\theta^2(1-m\eta)}, \tag{2.10}$$

where $\eta = \frac{\sigma_\theta^2}{\sigma_\theta^2 + \sigma_\epsilon^2} < 1$, respectively.

Among a population of rational traders and conservatism traders, λ denotes the fraction of this population being rational traders and $1 - \lambda$ denotes the fraction of this population being conservatism traders.

Noise traders' demand for the asset is normally distributed with the mean of zero and variance of σ_x^2. In addition, it is assumed that the total supply of the asset in the market is zero.

Hence, using Eqs. (2.9) and (2.10), the market clearing condition that equals the total demand for the asset to the total supply of the asset is described by:

$$\lambda\frac{\overline{\theta} + \eta\left(\theta + \epsilon - \overline{\theta}\right) - p}{a\sigma_\theta^2(1-\eta)} + (1-\lambda)\frac{\overline{\theta} + m\eta\left(\theta + \epsilon - \overline{\theta}\right) - p}{a\sigma_\theta^2(1-m\eta)} + x = 0. \tag{2.11}$$

In addition, the asset price is solved from Eq. (2.11) as:

$$p = \frac{-\left(\overline{\theta} + ax\sigma_\theta^2\right)(1-\eta)(1-m\eta) + S\eta\left(m(\eta-1) - \lambda(1-m)\right)}{\eta - 1 + \lambda\eta(m-1)}. \tag{2.12}$$

Note from Eq. (2.12) that $E(p) = \overline{\theta}$.

From Eqs. (2.9), (2.10) and (2.12), the demand functions of rational and conservatism traders are computed as:

$$X_r = \frac{1}{a\sigma_\theta^2\left(\eta - 1 + \lambda\eta(m-1)\right)}\left(ax\sigma_\theta^2\left(1 - m\eta\right) - \eta(1-m)(1-\lambda)\left(S - \overline{\theta}\right)\right), \tag{2.13}$$

and

$$X_c = \frac{1}{a\sigma_\theta^2\left(\eta - 1 + \lambda\eta(m-1)\right)}\left(ax\sigma_\theta^2\left(1 - \eta\right) + \lambda\eta(1-m)\left(S - \overline{\theta}\right)\right), \tag{2.14}$$

respectively[2].

In this model, the definition of the asset price overreaction or underreaction to new information is specified relative to the perfectly rational benchmark. Specifically,

---

[2] Equations (2.13) and (2.14) imply that $E(X_i) = 0$ for $i = r, c$.

the asset price overreaction to the new information occurs if in response to the new information, rational traders buy (sell) the asset and at the same time, the asset price is higher (lower) than what it would be in the market with rational traders and noise traders. In addition, the asset price underreaction to the new information occurs if in response to the new information, rational traders buy (sell) the asset and at the same time, the asset price is not as high (low) as it would be in the market with rational traders and noise traders.

2.3 The Asset Price Overreaction or Underreaction to New Information

This section analyzes how the conservatism bias causes the asset price to overreact or underreact to the good news or bad news.

Note from Eqs. (2.13) and (2.14) that if there are no noise traders in the market, then in responding to any informational signal, conservatism traders take trading positions opposite to rational traders (due to their conservatism biases). Hence, the asset price underreacts to the new information. With the presence of noise traders in the market, conservatism traders may not take trading positions opposite to rational traders. Depending on the realization of the signal and whether noise traders are net buyers or sellers of the asset, conservatism traders can take the trading positions on the same side as rational traders, and take larger trading positions than rational traders. Consequently, the asset price can overreact to the new information.

To ease the analysis to be conducted in the latter part of this section, the equations for $p - E_r(\theta\,|S)$ and $p - E_c(\theta\,|S)$ are computed from Eqs. (2.2), (2.6) and (2.12) as:

$$p - E_r(\theta\,|S) = \frac{\eta - 1}{\eta - 1 + \lambda\eta(m-1)}\left(ax\sigma_\theta^2(1 - m\eta) - \eta(1-m)(1-\lambda)(S - \overline{\theta})\right), \tag{2.15}$$

and

$$p - E_c(\theta\,|S) = \frac{m\eta - 1}{\eta - 1 + \lambda\eta(m-1)}\left(ax\sigma_\theta^2(1 - \eta) + \lambda\eta(1-m)(S - \overline{\theta})\right), \tag{2.16}$$

respectively.

In addition, taking the derivative with respect to m of Eq. (2.14) results in:

$$\frac{dX_c}{dm} = \frac{\lambda\eta(\eta - 1)(ax\sigma_\theta^2 - S + \overline{\theta})}{a\sigma_\theta^2(\eta - 1 + \lambda\eta(m-1))^2}. \tag{2.17}$$

Equation (2.17) shows how the change in the conservatism bias parameter affects the trading positions of conservatism traders. This equation is used in the analysis to be conducted later.

In addition, an informational signal is defined as good news if the informational signal is greater than or equal to the expected payoff of the asset, otherwise, it is defined as bad news. In addition, based on how far the informational signal is greater than the expected payoff of the asset, the good news is further classified as slightly good news if $\overline{\theta} \leq S < \overline{\theta} + a\,|x|\,\sigma_\theta^2$; very good news if $\overline{\theta} + a\,|x|\,\sigma_\theta^2 \leq S < \overline{\theta} + \frac{a|x|\sigma_\theta^2(1-m\eta)}{\eta(1-m)(1-\lambda)}$, where $\frac{1-m\eta}{\eta(1-m)(1-\lambda)} > 1$; and extremely good news if $S \geq \overline{\theta} + \frac{a|x|\sigma_\theta^2(1-m\eta)}{\eta(1-m)(1-\lambda)}$. Similarly, according to how far the informational signal is smaller than the expected payoff of the asset, bad news is further defined as slightly bad news if $\overline{\theta} - a\,|x|\,\sigma_\theta^2 \leq S < \overline{\theta}$; very bad news if $\overline{\theta} - \frac{a|x|\sigma_\theta^2(1-m\eta)}{\eta(1-m)(1-\lambda)} \leq S < \overline{\theta} - a\,|x|\,\sigma_\theta^2$; and extremely bad news if $S < \overline{\theta} - \frac{a|x|\sigma_\theta^2(1-m\eta)}{\eta(1-m)(1-\lambda)}$.

The following discusses how conservatism bias causes the asset price to overreact or underreact to different types of good news or bad news in the case of noise traders being net buyers or sellers of the asset. It begins with analyzing how the asset price reacts to the good news in the case of noise traders being net sellers of the asset.

If noise traders are net sellers (i.e., $x < 0$) of the asset, then in response to the good news, the asset price is priced below rational traders' conditional mean of the asset payoff (see Eq. (2.15)). Hence, rational traders buy the asset in response to the good news (due to Eq. (2.9)). On the other hand, conservatism traders may take trading positions either in the opposite direction to rational traders or on the same side as rational traders. If conservatism traders take trading positions opposite to rational traders, then the asset price is not as high as it would be in the market with rational traders and noise traders. If conservatism traders take a trading position on the same side as rational traders, then conservatism traders take smaller positions in buying the asset than rational traders (due to $X_c < X_r$ for $x < 0$ and $S \geq \overline{\theta}$ (see Eq. (2.17)). Consequently, the asset price is not as high as it would for the market with rational traders and noise traders. Thus, the asset price underreacts to the good news in the case of noise traders being net sellers of the asset.

On the other hand, if noise traders are net buyers of the asset, then conservatism traders sell the asset in response to all types of good news. However, whether conservatism traders take larger or smaller positions in selling the asset than rational traders depends on the type of good news. In addition, rational traders react differently to different types of good news. Hence, the following discussions are classified according to the type of good news into three cases: case (a), where the signal suggests slightly good news; case (b), where the signal suggests very good news and case (c), where the signal suggests extremely good news. In each case, detailed analysis is provided on how the asset price overreacts or underreacts to good news in the case of noise traders being net buyers of the asset. The following begins with the analysis in case (a).

Case (a): If the signal suggests slightly good news (i.e., $\overline{\theta} < S < \overline{\theta} + ax\sigma_\theta^2$), then the asset is priced above the conservatism traders' conditional mean of the asset payoff (see Eq. (2.16)). Hence, conservatism traders sell the asset in responding to slightly good news (see Eq. (2.10)). In addition, since $\frac{dX_c}{dm} < 0$ for $\overline{\theta} < S < \overline{\theta} + ax\sigma_\theta^2$ (see Eq. (2.17)), it follows that $0 > X_c > X_r$. Hence, in responding to the slightly good news, rational traders take larger positions in selling the asset than conservatism traders and the asset price is not as low as it would be in the market with rational traders and noise traders. That is, the asset price underreacts to the slightly good news in the case of noise traders being net buyers of the asset.

Case (b): If the signal suggests very good news (i.e., $\overline{\theta} + ax\sigma_\theta^2 < S < \overline{\theta} + \frac{ax\sigma_\theta^2(1-m\eta)}{\eta(1-m)(1-\lambda)}$, where $\frac{1-m\eta}{\eta(1-m)(1-\lambda)} > 1$), then the asset is priced above both rational and conservatism traders' conditional mean of the asset payoff (see Eqs. (2.15) and (2.16)). Hence, both rational and conservatism traders view the asset as overvalued and consequently, they both sell the asset (see Eqs. (2.9)and (2.10)). In addition, since $\frac{dX_c}{dm} > 0$ for $S > \overline{\theta} + ax\sigma_\theta^2$ (see Eq. (2.17)), it follows that $X_c < X_r$. Hence, conservatism traders take the larger positions in selling the asset than rational traders. It is the conservatism traders' aggressive selling the asset that pushes the asset price lower than what it would be in the market with rational traders and noise traders. That is, the asset price overreacts to very good news in the case of noise traders being net buyers.

Case (c): If the signal suggests extremely good news (i.e., $S > \overline{\theta} + \frac{ax\sigma_\theta^2(1-m\eta)}{\eta(1-m)(1-\lambda)}$), then rational traders buy the asset and conservatism traders sell the asset (see Eqs. (2.9), (2.10), (2.15) and (2.16)). Hence, conservatism traders' trading in a direction opposite to rational traders prevents the asset price from rising as high as it would in the market with rational traders and noise traders. That is, asset price underreacts to extremely good news in the case of noise traders being net buyers.

The following analyzes how conservatism traders cause the asset price to overreact or underreact to bad news. It begins with analysis in the case of noise traders being net buyers of the asset.

If noise traders are net buyers of the asset, then for all types of bad news, the asset is priced above rational traders' conditional mean of the asset payoff (see Eq. (2.15)). Hence, rational traders sell the asset for all types of bad news (see Eq. (2.9)). In addition, since $\frac{dX_c}{dm} < 0$ (see Eq. (2.17)), it follows that $X_c > X_r$. Also, note that conservatism traders either buy the asset or sell the asset. If conservatism traders buy the asset, then conservatism traders take trading positions opposite to rational traders. If conservatism traders sell the asset, then conservatism traders take smaller trading positions than rational traders (due to the inequality of $X_c > X_r$). In either case, conservatism traders prevent the asset price from being driven as low as it would in the market with rational traders and noise traders. That is, the asset price underreacts to all types of bad news in the case of noise traders being net buyers.

In addition, if noise traders are net sellers of the asset, then conservatism traders buy the asset in responding to all types of bad news. However, depending on the type of bad news, conservatism traders may take larger or smaller trading positions than rational traders do. Consequently, the asset price can overreact to one type of bad news and underreact to other types of bad news. Hence, based on the type of bad news, the following discussions are classified into three cases: case (d), where the signal suggests slightly bad news; case (e), where the signal suggests very bad news and case (f), where the signal suggests extremely bad news. In each case, detailed analysis is presented on how the conservatism bias causes the asset price to overreact or underreact to the bad news. The following begins with the analysis in case (d).

Case (d): If the signal suggests slightly bad news (i.e., $\overline{\theta} + ax\sigma_\theta^2 \leq S < \overline{\theta}$), then the asset is priced below the conservatism traders' conditional mean of the asset payoff (see Eq. (2.16)). Hence, conservatism traders buy the asset in response to slightly bad news (see Eq. (2.10)). In addition, since $\frac{dX_c}{dm} > 0$ (Eq. (2.17)), it follows that $0 < X_c < X_r$. Hence, in response to the slightly bad news, conservatism traders take smaller positions in buying the asset than rational traders. As a result, the asset price is not as high as it would be in the market with rational traders and noise traders. That is, the asset price underreacts to slightly bad news.

Case (e): If the signal suggests very bad news (i.e., $\overline{\theta} + \frac{ax\sigma_\theta^2(1-m\eta)}{\eta(1-m)(1-\lambda)} \leq S < \overline{\theta} + ax\sigma_\theta^2$), then the asset is priced below conservatism traders' conditional mean of the asset payoff (see Eq. (2.16)). Hence, in response to very bad news, conservatism traders buy the asset (see Eq. (2.10)). In addition, rational traders buy the asset in response to very bad news (see Eqs. (2.9) and (2.15)). Also, since $\frac{dX_c}{dm} < 0$ (see Eq. (2.17)), it follows that $X_c > X_r$. Hence, conservatism traders take larger positions in buying the asset than rational traders and the asset price is higher than what it would be in the market with rational traders and noise traders. That is, the asset price overreacts to very bad news.

Case (f): If the signal suggests extremely bad news (i.e., $S < \overline{\theta} + \frac{ax\sigma_\theta^2(1-m\eta)}{\eta(1-m)(1-\lambda)}$), then the asset is priced above the rational traders' conditional mean of the asset payoff (see Eq. (2.15)). Hence, rational traders sell the asset in responding to extremely bad news (see Eq. (2.9)). In addition, Eqs. (2.10) and (2.16) imply that conservatism traders buy the asset in response to extremely bad news. By trading in a direction opposite to rational traders, conservatism traders prevent the asset price from going as low as it would in the market with rational traders and noise traders. Hence, the asset price underreacts to extremely bad news.

The above results are formally stated in the proposition below:

Proposition 1 *In the competitive securities market, the following are true: (i) If noise traders are net sellers, then the asset price underreacts to all good news. (ii) If noise traders are net buyers, then the asset price underreacts to slightly good news and extremely good news; but overreacts to very good news. (iii) If noise traders are net buyers, then the asset price underreacts to all bad news. (iv) If noise traders are net sellers, then the asset price underreacts to slightly bad news and extremely bad news; but overreacts to very bad news.*

As can be seen from all above analyses, conservatism bias is the cause for the asset price to underreact or overreact to good news or bad news. In addition, more conservatism bias and/or larger subpopulation of conservatism traders (i.e., smaller m and/or smaller λ) can only exaggerate the impact on the asset price of conservatism bias in the same direction as it was with larger values of the parameters m and λ. As a result, the asset price underreaction or overreaction to new information becomes more severe.

2.4 Concluding Remarks

This chapter proves that conservatism bias is capable of generating asset price overreaction or underreaction to good news or bad news. These results are obtained in a static model of a competitive securities market with rational and conservatism traders and noise traders. The payoff of the asset is unknown, but rational and conservatism traders receive an informational signal about the asset payoff before any trade occurs. However, due to the conservatism bias, conservatism traders are slow to update their beliefs about the asset payoff relative to rational traders. In other words, if the informational signal is larger than the expected payoff of the asset, then a conservatism trader has a smaller conditional mean of the asset payoff than a rational trader does; in addition, if the informational signal is smaller than the expected payoff of the asset, then a conservatism trader has a larger conditional mean of the asset payoff than a rational trader does. As a result, with certain model parameter conditions, conservatism traders take the trading positions on the same side of the market as rational traders and, at the same time, take larger trading positions than rational traders. This results in the occurrence of asset price overreaction to the new information. On the other hand, with other model parameter conditions, conservatism traders take trading positions in a direction opposite to rational traders or on the same side of the market as rational traders, but take smaller trading positions than rational traders. This generates the occurrence of asset price underreaction to the new information.

Chapter 3
Conservatism Bias and Asset Price Overreaction or Underreaction to New Information in the Presence of Strategic Interaction

3.1 Introduction

This chapter examines how conservatism bias causes the asset price to overreact or underreact to new information in an asset market allowing for strategic interaction among traders. It proves that conservatism bias causes the asset price to overreact or underreact to different informational signals under different model parameter restrictions.

These results are obtained in a static model of an asset market. In the market, there are rational traders, conservatism traders and noise traders. The asset payoff is unknown to all traders; however, rational and conservatism traders receive an informational signal about the asset payoff before any trade takes place. Conservatism traders are slow to update their conditional mean of the asset payoff relative to rational traders. Rational and conservatism traders are both risk-neutral. Noise traders trade for their liquidity needs. Hence, their demand for the asset is assumed to be random. There is one market maker who supplies liquidity to the market. The cost of doing so is assumed to be zero. To maximize their own expected profits, all rational and conservatism traders strategically submit their market orders for the asset to the market maker. After observing the aggregate market orders for the asset of all traders, the market maker sets the asset price equal to the expected payoff of the asset conditional on the observed aggregate market orders for the asset of all traders. Note that the market maker does not observe the informational signal about the asset payoff.

In the equilibrium, the market order for the asset of each of rational and conservatism traders is generated from maximizing their expected profit, given the equilibrium market orders for the asset of all other traders and the equilibrium pricing rule. Given the equilibrium market orders for the asset of all traders, the asset price is equal to the expected payoff of the asset conditional on the observed aggregate demand for the asset of all traders. The asset price in the equilibrium is shown to be a linear function of the aggregate demand for the asset of all traders. For the sake of the following discussions, the coefficient of the aggregate demand for the asset of all traders in the asset pricing equation is referred to as the pricing parameter. This chapter finds that in the equilibrium, the asset price can overreact to some informational

G. Y. Luo, *Asset Price Response to New Information*, SpringerBriefs in Finance,
DOI 10.1007/978-1-4614-9369-3_3, © The Author(s) 2014

signals under certain model parameter value conditions and underreact to different informational signals under other model parameter value conditions.

The reasons for the asset price overreacting or underreacting to good news are as follows. Note that the derivative of the asset price with respect to the proportion of conservatism traders can be broken down into two components. One component is the impact on the asset price of noise traders' demand for the asset, which is the derivative (with respect to the proportion of conservatism traders) of the multiplication of the pricing parameter and noise traders' demand for the asset. Depending on model parameters, this component can be positive or negative. The other component is the impact on the asset price of the aggregate demand for the asset of rational and conservatism traders, which is defined as the derivative (with respect to the proportion of conservatism traders) of the multiplication of the pricing parameter and the aggregate demand for the asset of rational and conservatism traders. This impact is negative in the case of the signal suggesting good news. Hence, the net impact of these two components determines whether the derivative of the asset price (with respect to the proportion of conservatism traders) is positive or negative. If it is positive, then the asset price increases as the proportion of conservatism traders increases. In addition, note that rational traders buy the asset in response to the good news. Hence, the positive derivative of the asset price with respect to the proportion of conservatism traders, together with rational traders buying the asset in responding to the good news, implies that the asset price is higher than what it would be in the market with rational traders and noise traders, and the asset price overreacts to good news. In addition, if the derivative of the asset price with respect to the proportion of conservatism traders is negative, then the asset price decreases with the increase in the proportion of conservatism traders. Hence, the negative derivative of the asset price with respect to the proportion of conservatism traders, together with rational traders buying the asset in responding to good news, implies that the asset price is not as high as it would be in the market with rational traders and noise traders, and the asset price underreacts to good news.

Similar explanations would apply to explaining how conservatism bias causes the asset price to overreact or underreact to bad news.

The remainder of this chapter consists of three sections. The next section describes the model. Section 3 presents the results. Section 4 concludes the chapter.

3.2 The Model

Consider a static model of an asset market. The payoff for the asset (denoted as θ) is normally distributed with the mean $\overline{\theta}$ (where $\overline{\theta} > 0$) and variance of σ_θ^2. In the market, there are three types of traders: rational traders, conservatism traders and noise traders[1]. The payoff of the asset is unknown to all traders; however, rational and

[1] The presence of noise traders prevents the market maker from learning the informational signal perfectly.

conservatism traders receive an informational signal about the asset payoff before any trade occurs. The informational signal about the asset payoff (denoted as S) is modeled as: $S = \theta + \epsilon$, where ϵ is normally distributed with the mean of zero and variance of σ_ϵ^2; in addition, the random variable ϵ is independent of θ.

Rational traders, after receiving the informational signal, update their beliefs about the asset payoff according to:

$$E(\theta \,|(S,r)) = \overline{\theta} + \frac{\sigma_\theta^2}{\sigma_\theta^2 + \sigma_\epsilon^2}\left(S - \overline{\theta}\right), \tag{3.1}$$

where the parameter r indicates a rational trader. Note that Eq. (3.1) is derived from the results of Theorem 1 in the appendix by using the assumption that the random variables θ and ϵ are independently and normally distributed.

Conservatism traders exhibit conservatism bias. The conservatism bias is a type of behavioral bias identified in psychologists' experiments (see Edwards 1968). Traders with conservatism bias are slow to update their belief about the asset payoff relative to rational traders. Hence, conservatism traders' conditional mean of the asset payoff is modeled as:

$$E(\theta \,|(S,c)) = \overline{\theta} + m\left(E(\theta \,|(S,r)) - \overline{\theta}\right), \tag{3.2}$$

where the parameter c indicates a conservatism trader and $m \in (0,1)$. The parameter m captures the conservatism bias of the traders. The lower the parameter m, the greater is the conservatism bias of the traders.

Substituting Eq. (3.1) into (3.2) results in:

$$E(\theta \,|(S,c)) = \overline{\theta} + \frac{m\sigma_\theta^2}{\sigma_\theta^2 + \sigma_\epsilon^2}\left(S - \overline{\theta}\right). \tag{3.3}$$

Note from Eq. (3.3) that $E(\theta \,|(S,c)) \leq E(\theta \,|(S,r))$ if $S \geq \overline{\theta}$; and if $S < \overline{\theta}$, then $E(\theta \,|(S,c)) > E(\theta \,|(S,r))$. In other words, if the signal is greater than the expected payoff of the asset, then a conservatism trader has a smaller conditional mean of the asset payoff than a rational trader does; in addition, if the signal is smaller than the expected payoff of the asset, then a conservatism trader has a larger conditional mean of the asset payoff than a rational trader does.

Noise traders trade for their liquidity needs. Hence, their demand for the asset is assumed to be a normally distributed random variable (denoted as x) with the mean of zero and variance of σ_x^2. It is assumed that the random variables θ, ϵ and x are mutually independent.

There is a total of N rational and conservatism traders in the market. Among the N traders, the proportion of traders being conservatism traders is denoted as f, (where $f \in (0,1)$). In addition, there is one market maker in the market. The market maker supplies the liquidity to the market. The cost of doing so is assumed to be zero. After receiving the informational signal, all traders submit their market orders for the asset to the market maker. Hence, after observing the aggregate market orders for the asset (denoted as D) of all traders, the market maker sets the asset price (denoted as P) to equal to the conditional mean of the asset payoff. That is,

$$P = E(\theta \,|D). \tag{3.4}$$

The equilibrium is characterized by: (a) Given the asset pricing rule (described in Eq. (3.4)), by taking into account the impact of his market order on the asset price and on the market orders for the asset of other traders, trader i, where $i \in \{1, 2, .., N\}$, of type j, where $j \in \{r, h\}$, chooses his market order for the asset (denoted as X_{ij}) to solve

$$\max_{X_{ij}} \left[E(\theta \,|(S,j)) - E(P \left|(S,X_{ij})\right.)\right] X_{ij}, \tag{3.5}$$

where $E(\theta \,|(S, j)) = E(\theta \,|(S, r))$ if $j = r$; $E(\theta \,|(S, j)) = E(\theta \,|(S, h))$ if $j = h$, and $E(P \left|(S, X_{ij})\right.) = E(\theta \,|D)$. (b) Given the market orders for the asset of all traders, the market maker sets the asset price equal to the expected payoff of the asset conditional on the observed aggregate demand for the asset of all traders.

Denote N_r as the number of rational traders in the market and N_c as the number of conservatism traders in the market. Hence, $N = N_r + N_c$. Note that rational and conservatism traders are risk-neutral in this model.

In addition, assume that the equilibrium market orders for the asset of rational and conservatism traders are linear functions of their informational signal. That is, for $i = 1, 2, \ldots, N_r$,

$$X_{ir} = a_{ir} + b_{ir} S, \tag{3.6}$$

and for $i = 1, 2, .., N_c$,

$$X_{ic} = a_{ic} + b_{ic} S. \tag{3.7}$$

Also, the asset price is assumed to follow the linear pricing rule:

$$P = \mu + \lambda D, \tag{3.8}$$

where $D = \sum\limits_{i=1}^{N_r} X_{ir} + \sum\limits_{i=1}^{N_c} X_{ic} + x$. The following solves the equilibrium including all the coefficients μ, λ, a_{ir} and b_{ir} for $i = 1, 2, .., N_r$, and a_{ic} and b_{ic} for $i = 1, 2, .., N_c$.

With Eqs. (3.1), (3.3), (3.6), (3.7), and (3.8), optimization problem (3.5) is solved to generate the first-order conditions of optimization problem (3.5) as: for $\eta = \frac{\sigma_\theta^2}{\sigma_\theta^2 + \sigma_\epsilon^2}$,

$$\overline{\theta} + \eta \left(S - \overline{\theta}\right) - \mu - \lambda(2X_{ir} + \sum\nolimits_{\substack{n=1 \\ n \neq i}}^{N_r} (a_{nr} + b_{nr} S) + \sum\nolimits_{n=1}^{N_c} (a_{nc} + b_{nc} S)) = 0, \tag{3.9}$$

and

$$\overline{\theta} + m\eta \left(S - \overline{\theta}\right) - \mu - \lambda(2X_{ic} + \sum\nolimits_{n=1}^{N_r} (a_{nr} + b_{nr} S) + \sum\nolimits_{\substack{n=1 \\ n \neq i}}^{N_c} (a_{nc} + b_{nc} S)) = 0. \tag{3.10}$$

In addition, substituting Eqs. (3.6) and (3.7) into Eqs. (3.9) and (3.10) results in:

$$a_{ij} = \frac{\overline{\theta} - \mu - R_j \eta \overline{\theta}}{\lambda} - A, \tag{3.11}$$

and

$$b_{ij} = \frac{R_j \eta}{\lambda} - B, \tag{3.12}$$

where $A = \sum_{n=1}^{N_r} a_{nr} + \sum_{n=1}^{N_c} a_{nc}$; $B = \sum_{n=1}^{N_r} b_{nr} + \sum_{n=1}^{N_c} b_{nc}$; $R_j = 1$ if $j = r$; and $R_j = m$, if $j = c$.

Note from Eqs. (3.11) and (3.12) that for $i^{'} \neq i$, $a_{ij} = a_{i^{'}j}$ and $b_{ij} = b_{i^{'}j}$ for $j \in \{r, c\}$. Hence, denote $a_r = a_{ir}$, $b_r = b_{ir}$ for $i = 1, 2, .., N_r$; and denote $a_c = a_{ic}$, $b_c = b_{ic}$ for $i = 1, 2, .., N_c$. Note that the coefficients a_r, b_r, a_c, and b_c are computed from Eqs. (3.11) and (3.12) as:

$$a_r = \frac{\overline{\theta} - \mu + \eta\overline{\theta}(Nf(m-1) - 1)}{\lambda(N+1)}, \tag{3.13}$$

$$a_c = \frac{\overline{\theta} - \mu + \eta\overline{\theta}(N(1-f)(1-m) - m)}{\lambda(N+1)}, \tag{3.14}$$

$$b_r = \frac{\eta(1 + Nf(1-m))}{\lambda(N+1)}, \tag{3.15}$$

and

$$b_c = \frac{\eta(m - N(1-f)(1-m))}{\lambda(N+1)}, \tag{3.16}$$

respectively.

Also, the asset price is computed from Eq. (3.4) as:

$$\begin{aligned} P &= E\left(\theta \,|A + BS + x = D\right) \\ &= \overline{\theta} + \frac{B\sigma_\theta^2}{B^2\sigma_S^2 + \sigma_x^2}(D - A - B\overline{\theta}). \end{aligned} \tag{3.17}$$

In addition, using Eqs. (3.8) and (3.17) along with the definitions of A and B, one can show that

$$\mu = \overline{\theta}, \tag{3.18}$$

and

$$\lambda^2 = \frac{N\eta\sigma_\theta^2(fm - f + 1)(Nf(1-m) + 1)}{\sigma_x^2(1+N)^2}. \tag{3.19}$$

Note from Eq. (3.19) that there is one positive solution and one negative solution for the parameter λ. To ensure that the equilibrium asset price increases with the increases in the total demand for the asset and also to ensure that the second-order conditions of optimization problem (3.5) hold, the positive solution from Eq. (3.19) is used for the parameter λ.

Note that all traders of the same type have the same market orders for the asset. Hence, denote the market orders for the asset of rational and conservatism traders as X_r and X_c, respectively. Therefore, using Eqs. (3.6), (3.7), (3.8), (3.13) through (3.16), and (3.18), the equilibrium market orders for the asset of rational and conservatism traders and the equilibrium asset price are computed as:

$$X_r = \frac{\eta(Nf(1-m)+1)(S-\overline{\theta})}{\lambda(N+1)}, \tag{3.20}$$

$$X_c = \frac{\eta\,[N(m-1)(1-f)+m)]\,(S-\overline{\theta})}{\lambda(N+1)}, \tag{3.21}$$

and

$$P = \overline{\theta} + \lambda x + \frac{N\eta(1-f+fm)(S-\overline{\theta})}{N+1}, \tag{3.22}$$

respectively, where λ is described in Eq. (3.19).

The informational signal is considered as good news if $S \geq \overline{\theta}$; otherwise, it is considered as bad news. Note from Eq. (3.20) that rational traders buy the asset if the signal indicates good news; and if the informational signal suggests bad news, then rational traders sell the asset. In addition, Eq. (3.21) suggests that depending on the model parameter values, conservatism traders may buy or sell the asset in response to the good news or bad news.

Also, note from Eqs. (3.1) and (3.3) that with the conservatism bias parameter less than one, a conservatism trader has a smaller demand for the asset than a rational trader does in the case of the signal suggesting good news; in addition, a conservatism trader has a larger demand for the asset than a rational trader does in the case of the signal suggesting bad news.

3.3 The Asset Price Reaction to New Information

This section examines how conservatism bias causes the asset price to overreact or underreact to good news or bad news. To ease the analysis to be conducted in the latter part of this section, some definitions are first specified below:

In this model, the asset price overreaction to new information occurs if in response to the new information, rational traders buy (sell) the asset and at the same time, the asset price is higher (lower) than what it would be in the market with rational traders and noise traders; on the other hand, the asset price underreaction to the new information occurs if in response to the new information, rational traders buy (sell) the asset and at the same time, the asset price is not as high (low) as it would be in the market with rational traders and noise traders.

In addition, the equations for the derivative (with respect to the proportion of conservatism traders) of the parameter λ and the asset price are computed from Eqs. (3.19) and (3.22) as:

$$\frac{d\lambda}{df} = \frac{N\eta\sigma_\theta^2\,(1-m)\,(N-2Nf+2Nfm-1)}{2\lambda\,(N+1)^2\,\sigma_x^2}, \tag{3.23}$$

and

$$\frac{dP}{df} = x\frac{d\lambda}{df} - \frac{N\eta(1-m)(S-\overline{\theta})}{N+1}, \tag{3.24}$$

respectively.

Note from Eq. (3.23) that with the increase in the proportion of conservatism traders, the parameter λ increases if $N-2Nf+2Nfm-1>0$ (or $f<\frac{N-1}{2\,N(1-m)}$) and it decreases if $N-2Nf+2Nfm-1<0$ (or $f>\frac{N-1}{2\,N(1-m)}$ and $m<\frac{1}{2}+\frac{1}{2\,N}$).

Also, note from Eq. (3.24) that the derivative of the asset price with respect to f can be broken into two components. One component is the first term on the right hand side of Eq. (3.24), which is the impact on the asset price of noise traders' demand for the asset. This component depends on noise traders' demand for the asset and the derivative of the parameter λ with respect to f. The other component is the second term of the right hand side of Eq. (3.24), which is the impact on the asset price of the aggregate demand for the asset of rational and conservatism traders. This impact does not change as the proportion of conservatism traders increases. If both components are positive, then the asset price increases as the proportion of conservatism traders increases. If both components are negative, then the asset price decreases as the proportion of conservatism traders increases. If one of the components is positive and the other is negative, then depending on which component dominates the other, the net effect can be positive or negative.

In addition, substituting Eq. (3.23) into (3.24) results in:

$$\frac{dP}{df} = \frac{N\eta(1-m)\left[x\sigma_\theta^2(N-2Nf+2Nfm-1)-2\lambda(N+1)\sigma_x^2(S-\overline{\theta})\right]}{2\lambda(N+1)^2\sigma_x^2}. \tag{3.25}$$

The following provides detailed discussions on how conservatism bias causes the asset price to overreact or underreact to good news or bad news. The discussions are classified into four scenarios according to whether the signal indicates good news or bad news and whether noise traders are net buyers or sellers of the asset. The following begins with the analysis on how the asset price reacts to good news in the case of noise traders being net buyers of the asset.

Scenario (a): the informational signal suggests good news and noise traders are net buyers of the asset

Note from Eq. (3.20) that rational traders buy the asset in response to the good news. Rational traders' buying the asset together with the sign of the derivative of the asset price with respect to the proportion of conservatism traders determines whether the asset price overreacts or underreacts to the good news.

Specifically, if $N - 2Nf + 2Nfm - 1 < 0$ (or $f > \frac{N-1}{2\,N(1-m)}$ and $m < \frac{1}{2} + \frac{1}{2\,N}$), then the asset price decreases as the proportion of conservatism traders increases (i.e, $\frac{dP}{df} < 0$) (see Eq. (3.25)). Note that the negative sign of $\frac{dP}{df}$ suggests that asset price is not as high as it would be in the market with rational traders and noise traders. Hence, the negative sign of the derivative of the asset price with respect to the proportion of conservatism traders, together with rational traders buying the asset in response to the good news, implies that the asset price underreacts to the good news.

In addition, if $N - 2Nf + 2Nfm - 1 > 0$ (or $f < \frac{N-1}{2\,N(1-m)}$), then $\frac{dP}{df} > 0$ for $\overline{\theta} < S < \overline{\theta} + \frac{x\sigma_\theta^2(N-2Nf+2Nfm-1)}{2\lambda(N+1)\sigma_x^2}$ (see Eq. (3.25)). Note that the positive sign of $\frac{dP}{df}$ indicates that the asset price is higher than what it would be in the market with rational traders and noise traders. Hence, the positive sign of $\frac{dP}{df}$, together with rational traders buying the asset in response to the good news, implies that the asset price overreacts to the good news with $\overline{\theta} < S < \overline{\theta} + \frac{x\sigma_\theta^2(N-2Nf+2Nfm-1)}{2\lambda(N+1)\sigma_x^2}$.

Also, note from Eq. (3.25) that $\frac{dP}{df} < 0$ if $N - 2Nf + 2Nfm - 1 > 0$ (or $f < \frac{N-1}{2\,N(1-m)}$) and $S > \overline{\theta} + \frac{x\sigma_\theta^2(N-2Nf+2Nfm-1)}{2\lambda(N+1)\sigma_x^2}$. Hence, the negative sign of $\frac{dP}{df}$, together with rational traders buying the asset in response to the good news, implies that the asset price is not as high as it would be in the market with rational traders and noise traders and the asset price underreacts to the good news with $S > \overline{\theta} + \frac{x\sigma_\theta^2(N-2Nf+2Nfm-1)}{2\lambda(N+1)\sigma_x^2}$.

Scenario (b): the informational signal suggests good news and noise traders are net sellers of the asset

Eq. (3.25) suggests that $\frac{dP}{df} < 0$ if $N - 2Nf + 2Nfm - 1 < 0$ (or $f > \frac{N-1}{2\,N(1-m)}$ and $m < \frac{1}{2} + \frac{1}{2\,N}$), $S > \overline{\theta} + \frac{x\sigma_\theta^2(N-2Nf+2Nfm-1)}{2\lambda(N+1)\sigma_x^2}$, and $\overline{\theta} + \lambda x > 0$ (ensuring a positive asset price (see Eq. (3.22)). In addition, note from Eq. (3.20) that rational traders buy the asset in response to the good news. Hence, the negative sign of $\frac{dP}{df}$, together with rational traders buying the asset in response to the good news, implies that the asset price is not as high as it would be in the market with rational traders and noise traders, and the asset price underreacts to the good news with $S > \overline{\theta} + \frac{x\sigma_\theta^2(N-2Nf+2Nfm-1)}{2\lambda(N+1)\sigma_x^2}$.

In addition, Eq. (3.25) suggests that $\frac{dP}{df} > 0$ if $N - 2Nf + 2Nfm - 1 < 0$ (or $f > \frac{N-1}{2\,N(1-m)}$ and $m < \frac{1}{2} + \frac{1}{2\,N}$), $\overline{\theta} < S < \overline{\theta} + \frac{x\sigma_\theta^2(N-2Nf+2Nfm-1)}{2\lambda(N+1)\sigma_x^2}$ and $\overline{\theta} + \lambda x > 0$ (ensuring a positive asset price (see Eq. (3.22)). Hence, the positive sign of $\frac{dP}{df}$, together with rational traders buying the asset in responding to the good news, implies that the asset price is higher than what it would be in the market with rational traders and noise traders, and the asset price overreacts to the good news with $\overline{\theta} < S < \overline{\theta} + \frac{x\sigma_\theta^2(N-2Nf+2Nfm-1)}{2\lambda(N+1)\sigma_x^2}$.

Also, Eq. (3.25) suggests that $\frac{dP}{df} < 0$ if $N - 2Nf + 2Nfm - 1 > 0$ (or $f < \frac{N-1}{2\,N(1-m)}$) and $\overline{\theta} + \lambda x > 0$ (ensuring a positive asset price (see Eq. (3.22)). Hence, the negative sign of $\frac{dP}{df}$, together with rational traders buying the asset price in response to the good news, implies that the asset price is not as high as it would be in the market with rational traders and noise traders, and the asset price underreacts to the good news.

Scenarios (c) and (d) below provide the brief analysis on how conservatism bias causes the asset price to overreact or underreact to bad news.

Scenario (c): the informational signal indicates bad news and noise traders are net buyers of the asset

Note from Eq. (3.25) that $\frac{dP}{df} > 0$ if $N-2Nf+2Nfm-1 > 0$ (or $f < \frac{N-1}{2\,N(1-m)}$) and $\overline{\theta} > S > \overline{\theta} - \frac{(N+1)(\overline{\theta}+\lambda x)}{N\eta(1-f+fm)}$ (ensuring a positive asset price (see Eq. (3.22)). In addition, note from Eq. (3.20) that in response to the bad news, rational traders sell the asset. Hence, the positive sign of $\frac{dP}{df}$, together with rational traders selling the asset in response to the bad news, indicates that the asset price is not as low as it would be in the market with rational traders and noise traders, and the asset price underreacts to the bad news with $\overline{\theta} > S > \overline{\theta} - \frac{(N+1)(\overline{\theta}+\lambda x)}{N\eta(1-f+fm)}$.

In addition, note from Eq. (3.25) that $\frac{dP}{df} > 0$ if $N-2Nf+2Nfm-1 < 0$ (or $f > \frac{N-1}{2\,N(1-m)}$ and $m < \frac{1}{2}+\frac{1}{2\,N}$) and $\overline{\theta}-\frac{(N+1)(\overline{\theta}+\lambda x)}{N\eta(1-f+fm)} < S < \overline{\theta}+\frac{x\sigma_\theta^2(N-2Nf+2Nfm-1)}{2\lambda(N+1)\sigma_x^2}$, where $\frac{x\sigma_\theta^2(N-2Nf+2Nfm-1)}{2\lambda(N+1)\sigma_x^2} > -\frac{(N+1)(\overline{\theta}+\lambda x)}{N\eta(1-f+fm)}$ (ensuring a positive asset price (see Eq. (3.22)). Hence, the positive derivative of the asset price with respect to the proportion of conservatism traders, together with rational traders selling the asset price in response to the bad news, implies that the asset price is not as low as it would be in the market with rational traders and noise traders, and the asset price underreacts to the bad news with $\overline{\theta} - \frac{(N+1)(\overline{\theta}+\lambda x)}{N\eta(1-f+fm)} < S < \overline{\theta} + \frac{x\sigma_\theta^2(N-2Nf+2Nfm-1)}{2\lambda(N+1)\sigma_x^2}$.

Also, note from Eq. (3.25) that $\frac{dP}{df} < 0$ if $N - 2Nf + 2Nfm - 1 < 0$ (or $f > \frac{N-1}{2\,N(1-m)}$ and $m < \frac{1}{2} + \frac{1}{2\,N}$) and $\overline{\theta} > S > \overline{\theta} + \frac{x\sigma_\theta^2(N-2Nf+2Nfm-1)}{2\lambda(N+1)\sigma_x^2}$, where $\frac{x\sigma_\theta^2(N-2Nf+2Nfm-1)}{2\lambda(N+1)\sigma_x^2} > -\frac{(N+1)(\overline{\theta}+\lambda x)}{N\eta(1-f+fm)}$ (ensuring a positive asset price (see Eq. (3.22))). Hence, the negative sign of $\frac{dP}{df}$, together with rational traders selling the asset in responding to the bad news, implies that the asset price is lower than what it would be in the market with rational traders and noise traders, and the asset price overreacts to the bad news with $\overline{\theta} > S > \overline{\theta} + \frac{x\sigma_\theta^2(N-2Nf+2Nfm-1)}{2\lambda(N+1)\sigma_x^2}$.

Scenario (d): the informational signal indicates bad news and noise traders are net sellers of the asset

Due to Eq. (3.25), $\frac{dP}{df} > 0$ if $N - 2Nf + 2Nfm - 1 < 0$ (or $f > \frac{N-1}{2\,N(1-m)}$ and $m < \frac{1}{2} + \frac{1}{2\,N}$), $\overline{\theta} > S > \overline{\theta} - \frac{(N+1)(\overline{\theta}+\lambda x)}{N\eta(1-f+fm)}$ and $\overline{\theta} + \lambda x > 0$ (ensuring a positive asset price (see Eq. (3.22)). In addition, note from Eq. (3.20) that in response to the bad news, rational traders sell the asset. Hence, the positive sign of $\frac{dP}{df}$, together with rational traders selling the asset in response to the bad news, implies that the asset price underreacts to the bad news with $\overline{\theta} > S > \overline{\theta} - \frac{(N+1)(\overline{\theta}+\lambda x)}{N\eta(1-f+fm)}$.

In addition, note from Eq. (3.25) that $\frac{dP}{df} < 0$ if $N - 2Nf + 2Nfm - 1 > 0$ (or $f < \frac{N-1}{2\,N(1-m)}$), and $\overline{\theta} > S > \overline{\theta} + \frac{x\sigma_\theta^2(N-2Nf+2Nfm-1)}{2\lambda(N+1)\sigma_x^2}$, where $\frac{x\sigma_\theta^2(N-2Nf+2Nfm-1)}{2\lambda(N+1)\sigma_x^2} > -\frac{(N+1)(\overline{\theta}+\lambda x)}{N\eta(1-f+fm)}$ (ensuring a positive asset price (see Eq. (3.22))). Hence, the negative sign of $\frac{dP}{df}$, together with rational traders selling the asset in response to the bad news (see Eq. (3.20)), implies that the asset price overreacts to the bad news with $\overline{\theta} > S > \overline{\theta} + \frac{x\sigma_\theta^2(N-2Nf+2Nfm-1)}{2\lambda(N+1)\sigma_x^2}$.

Also, note from Eq. (3.25) that $\frac{dP}{df} > 0$ if $N - 2Nf + 2Nfm - 1 > 0$ (or $f < \frac{N-1}{2\,N(1-m)}$) and $\overline{\theta} - \frac{(N+1)(\overline{\theta}+\lambda x)}{N\eta(1-f+fm)} < S < \overline{\theta} + \frac{x\sigma_\theta^2(N-2Nf+2Nfm-1)}{2\lambda(N+1)\sigma_x^2}$, where $\frac{x\sigma_\theta^2(N-2Nf+2Nfm-1)}{2\lambda(N+1)\sigma_x^2} > -\frac{(N+1)(\overline{\theta}+\lambda x)}{N\eta(1-f+fm)}$ (ensuring a positive asset price (see Eq. (3.22))). Hence, the positive derivative of the asset price with respect to the proportion of conservatism traders, together with rational traders selling the asset in response to the bad news (see Eq. (3.20)), implies that the asset price is not as low as it would be in the market with rational traders and noise traders, and the asset price underreacts to the bad news with $\overline{\theta} - \frac{(N+1)(\overline{\theta}+\lambda x)}{N\eta(1-f+fm)} < S < \overline{\theta} + \frac{x\sigma_\theta^2(N-2Nf+2Nfm-1)}{2\lambda(N+1)\sigma_x^2}$.

In summary, the results in the scenarios (a), (b), (c), and (d) suggest that conservatism bias causes the asset price to overreact or underreact to good news or bad news. Proposition 1 below presents the results in scenarios (a) and (c) where noise traders are net buyers of the asset.

Proposition 1 *If noise traders are net buyers of the asset, then the following statements are true: (a) If* $f > \frac{N-1}{2\,N(1-m)}$ *and* $m < \frac{1}{2} + \frac{1}{2\,N}$*, then (i) the asset price underreacts to the good news; (ii) with* $\frac{x\sigma_\theta^2(N-2Nf+2Nfm-1)}{2\lambda(N+1)\sigma_x^2} > -\frac{(N+1)(\overline{\theta}+\lambda x)}{N\eta(1-f+fm)}$*, the asset price underreacts to the bad news with* $\overline{\theta} - \frac{(N+1)(\overline{\theta}+\lambda x)}{N\eta(1-f+fm)} < S < \overline{\theta} + \frac{x\sigma_\theta^2(N-2Nf+2Nfm-1)}{2\lambda(N+1)\sigma_x^2}$ *and overreacts to the bad news with* $\overline{\theta} > S > \overline{\theta} + \frac{x\sigma_\theta^2(N-2Nf+2Nfm-1)}{2\lambda(N+1)\sigma_x^2}$*. (b) If* $f < \frac{N-1}{2\,N(1-m)}$*, then (i) the asset price overreacts to the good news with* $\overline{\theta} < S < \overline{\theta} + \frac{x\sigma_\theta^2(N-2Nf+2Nfm-1)}{2\lambda(N+1)\sigma_x^2}$ *and underreacts to the good news with* $S > \overline{\theta} + \frac{x\sigma_\theta^2(N-2Nf+2Nfm-1)}{2\lambda(N+1)\sigma_x^2}$*; (ii) the asset price underreacts to the bad news with* $\overline{\theta} > S > \overline{\theta} - \frac{(N+1)(\overline{\theta}+\lambda x)}{N\eta(1-f+fm)}$.

The results in scenarios (b) and (d), where noise traders are net sellers of the asset, are formally stated in Proposition 2 below:

Proposition 2 *If noise traders are net sellers of the asset, then the following statements are true: (a) If* $f > \frac{N-1}{2\,N(1-m)}$*,* $m < \frac{1}{2} + \frac{1}{2\,N}$*, and* $\overline{\theta} + \lambda x > 0$*, then (i) the asset price overreacts to the good news with* $\overline{\theta} < S < \overline{\theta} + \frac{x\sigma_\theta^2(N-2Nf+2Nfm-1)}{2\lambda(N+1)\sigma_x^2}$ *and* *underreacts to the good news with* $S > \overline{\theta} + \frac{x\sigma_\theta^2(N-2Nf+2Nfm-1)}{2\lambda(N+1)\sigma_x^2}$*; (ii) the asset price underreacts to the bad news with* $\overline{\theta} > S > \overline{\theta} - \frac{(N+1)(\overline{\theta}+\lambda x)}{N\eta(1-f+fm)}$*. (b) If* $f < \frac{N-1}{2\,N(1-m)}$*, then (i) with* $\overline{\theta} + \lambda x > 0$*, the asset price underreacts to the good news; (ii) with* $\frac{x\sigma_\theta^2(N-2Nf+2Nfm-1)}{2\lambda(N+1)\sigma_x^2} > -\frac{(N+1)(\overline{\theta}+\lambda x)}{N\eta(1-f+fm)}$*, the asset price underreacts to the bad news with* $\overline{\theta} - \frac{(N+1)(\overline{\theta}+\lambda x)}{N\eta(1-f+fm)} < S < \overline{\theta} + \frac{x\sigma_\theta^2(N-2Nf+2Nfm-1)}{2\lambda(N+1)\sigma_x^2}$ *and overreacts to the bad news with* $\overline{\theta} > S > \overline{\theta} + \frac{x\sigma_\theta^2(N-2Nf+2Nfm-1)}{2\lambda(N+1)\sigma_x^2}$*.*

The results of Proposition 1 and 2 suggest that conservatism bias causes the asset price to overreact or underreact to good news or bad news.

3.4 Concluding Remarks

This chapter shows analytically that conservatism bias causes the asset price to overreact or underreact to good news or bad news. These results are obtained in a static model of an asset market. In the asset market, the payoff of the asset is unknown to traders, but rational and conservatism traders receive an informational signal about the asset payoff before any trade takes place. Due to the conservatism bias, conservatism traders are slow to update their belief about the asset payoff relative to rational traders. Hence, if the signal is greater than the expected payoff of the asset, then a conservatism trader has a smaller conditional mean of the asset payoff than a rational trader does; in addition, if the signal is smaller than the expected payoff of the asset, then a conservatism trader has a larger conditional mean of the asset payoff. Rational and conservatism traders submit their market orders for the asset strategically to the market maker to maximize their own expected profits. After observing the aggregate demand for the asset of all traders, the market maker sets the asset price equal to the expected payoff of the asset conditional on the observed aggregate demand for the asset of all traders.

This chapter shows that whether the asset price overreacts or underreacts to the new information depends on whether rational traders buy or sell the asset in response to the new information and whether the derivative of the asset price with respect to the proportion of conservatism traders is positive or negative.

This chapter proves that conservatism bias causes the asset price to overreact to some informational signals under some model parameter restrictions and underreact to the other informational signals under different model parameter restrictions.

Chapter 4
Representativeness Heuristic and Asset Price Overreaction or Underreaction to New Information in a Competitive Securities Market

4.1 Introduction

This chapter examines how representativeness heuristic causes the asset price to overreact or underreact to good news or bad news.

Specifically, this chapter constructs a static model of a competitive securities market. In the market, there are two assets: risk-free asset and risky asset. The payoff of the risk-free asset is one and the payoff of the risky asset is normally distributed. In addition, there are three types of traders: rational traders, heuristic traders and noise traders. Noise traders trade for their liquidity reasons. Hence, noise traders' demand for the asset is assumed to be random. Heuristic traders exhibit representativeness heuristic. Before any trade occurs, rational and heuristic traders receive an informational signal about the asset payoff. Due to the representativeness heuristic, heuristic traders place too much weight on the new information and not enough weight on their prior knowledge. In other words, if the signal is greater (smaller) than the expected payoff of the asset, then a heuristic trader has a larger (smaller) conditional mean of the asset than a rational trader does; in addition, for any given informational signal, a heuristic trader has a smaller conditional variance of the asset payoff than a rational trader does. Both rational and heuristic traders have an exponential utility function. In the competitive securities market, traders take the asset price as given.

The asset price underreaction or overreaction to the new information in this model are defined relative to a perfectly rational benchmark. In other words, the asset price overreaction to the new information occurs if in response to the new information, rational traders buy (sell) the asset and at the same time, the asset price is higher (lower) than what it would be in the market with rational traders and noise traders; otherwise, the asset price underreaction to the new information occurs.

In this model, an informational signal is considered as good news if the signal is greater than the expected payoff of the asset; otherwise, it is considered as bad news. If the informational signal is far greater (smaller) than the expected payoff of the asset, then the informational signal is considered as extremely good news (extremely bad news). In addition, if the informational signal suggests good news (bad news) with its signal close to the expected payoff of the asset, then the informational signal is considered as slightly good news (slightly bad news).

G. Y. Luo, *Asset Price Response to New Information,* SpringerBriefs in Finance,
DOI 10.1007/978-1-4614-9369-3_4, © The Author(s) 2014

The results of this chapter shows that regardless of noise traders being net buyers or sellers of the asset, the representativeness heuristic causes the asset price to underreact to the extremely good news (or extremely bad news) and to overreact to the slightly good news (or slightly bad news).

The intuition for the asset price underreaction to the extremely good news is as follows. Note that with noise traders being net sellers of the asset, heuristic traders buy the asset in response to the good news. The reason for heuristic traders buying the asset is that with the signal suggesting the good news, a heuristic trader has a larger conditional mean of the asset payoff than a rational trader does. If the signal suggests extremely good news, then heuristic traders' positions in buying the asset are very large and the asset price is driven too high. Hence, rational traders profit from trading in a direction opposite to heuristic traders. Therefore, the asset price is not as low as it would be in the market with rational traders and noise traders. That is, the asset price underreacts to the extremely good news.

In addition, note that with noise traders being net buyers of the asset, rational traders sell the asset in responding to the good news. The reason for rational traders selling the asset is that in the case of the signal suggesting the good news, a rational trader has a smaller conditional mean of the asset payoff than a heuristic trader does. If the signal suggests extremely good news, then rational traders' positions in selling the asset are very large and the asset price is driven too low. Hence, heuristic traders profit from trading in a direction opposite to rational traders. As a result, the asset price is not as low as it would be in the market with rational traders and noise traders. That is, the asset price underreacts to the extremely good news.

Therefore, regardless of noise traders being net sellers or buyers of the asset, due to the representativeness heuristic, the asset price underreacts to the extremely good news.

Similar intuition can be used to explain the cause of the asset underreaction to extremely bad news.

The intuition for the asset price overreaction to the slightly good news is as follows. Note that with noise traders being net sellers of the asset, heuristic traders buy the asset in response to the good news. The reason for heuristic traders buying the asset is that in the case of the signal suggesting good news, a heuristic trader has a larger conditional mean of the asset payoff than a rational trader does. If the signal suggests slightly good news, then heuristic traders' positions in buying the asset are not as big as in the previous case in which the signal suggests extremely good news. Consequently, the asset price is not driven as high as in that case and rational traders profit from trading on the same side as heuristic traders. Note that in the case of the signal suggesting good news, a heuristic trader has a larger conditional mean of the asset payoff than a rational trader does. Hence, heuristic traders take larger positions in buying the asset than rational traders and the asset price is higher than what it would be in the market with rational traders and noise traders. Thus, the asset price overreacts to the slightly good news.

In addition, note that with noise traders being net buyers of the asset, rational traders sell the asset in response to the good news. The reason for rational traders selling the asset is that in the case of the signal suggesting good news, a rational trader has a smaller conditional mean of the asset payoff than a heuristic trader does.

If the signal suggests slightly good news, then rational traders' positions in selling the asset are not as big as in the previous case in which the signal suggests extremely good news. Hence, the asset price is not as low as in that case and heuristic traders profit from trading on the same side as rational traders. Note that for any given informational signal, a heuristic trader has a smaller conditional variance of the asset payoff than a rational trader does. Hence, heuristic traders take larger positions in selling the asset than rational traders. As a result, the asset price is lower than what it would be in the market with rational traders and noise traders. That is, the asset price overreacts to the slightly good news.

Regardless of noise traders being net buyers or sellers of the asset, due to the representativeness heuristic, the asset price overreacts to the slightly good news.

Similar intuition can be used to explain the cause of the asset price overreaction to slightly bad news.

Given the importance of the representativeness heuristic in financial markets, Fischer and Verrecchia (1999) examine whether traders with the representativeness heuristic would survive in the long run. They find that heuristic traders overreact to their private information and have aggressive trading behavior. Heuristic traders' aggressive trading behavior in turn causes them to capture more information rent and earn higher utility. Therefore, heuristic traders survive in the long run. Luo (2013) shows that the existence of noise traders creates room for heuristic traders to survive. This is because heuristic traders can derive more expected profit from misvaluation (created by noise traders) than rational traders, consequently, they survive in the long run.

The remainder of this chapter consists of three sections. Section 2 presents the model. The analysis and results are contained in Sect. 3 and Sect. 4 provides some concluding remarks.

4.2 The Model

This section presents a static model of a competitive securities market. In the market, there are two assets: risk-free asset and risky asset. The payoff of the risk-free asset is one and the payoff of the risky asset (denoted as θ) is normally distributed with the mean of $\overline{\theta}$, where $\overline{\theta} > 0$, and variance of σ_θ^2. Also, in the market, there are three types of traders: rational traders, heuristic traders and noise traders. Noise traders trade for their liquidity reasons. Hence, noise traders' demand for the asset (denoted as x) is assumed to be normally distributed with the mean of zero and variance of σ_x^2.

Before any trade takes place, rational and heuristic traders receive an informational signal (denoted as S) about the asset payoff. The informational signal S is modeled as: $S = \theta + \epsilon$, where the residual error ϵ is normally distributed with the mean of zero and variance of σ_ϵ^2. It is assumed that ϵ is independent of θ. Based on the informational signal received, rational traders compute their conditional mean and variance of the asset payoff according to:

$$E_r(\theta \mid S) = \overline{\theta} + \frac{\sigma_\theta^2}{\sigma_\theta^2 + \sigma_\epsilon^2}\left(S - \overline{\theta}\right), \tag{4.1}$$

and

$$Var_r(\theta\,|S) = \sigma_\theta^2 - \frac{\sigma_\theta^4}{\sigma_\theta^2 + \sigma_\epsilon^2} = \frac{\sigma_\theta^2\sigma_\epsilon^2}{\sigma_\theta^2 + \sigma_\epsilon^2}, \tag{4.2}$$

respectively, where subscript r indicates a rational trader. Note that Eqs. (4.1) and (4.2) are derived from the results of Theorem 1 in the appendix[1].

Heuristic traders exhibit representativeness heuristic. The representativeness heuristic is well-documented in psychology literature as a behavioral bias (see Kahneman and Tversky 1973; Tversky and Kahneman 1974; Grether 1980). Traders with the representativeness heuristic place too much weight on new information and not enough weight on their prior knowledge[2]. Hence, it is assumed that for any given informational signal, the conditional mean and variance of the asset payoff for heuristic traders are modeled as:

$$E_h(\theta\,|S) = \overline{\theta} + m\left(E_r(\theta\,|S) - \overline{\theta}\right), \tag{4.3}$$

and

$$Var_h(\theta\,|S) = \sigma_\theta^2 + m\left(Var_r(\theta\,|S) - \sigma_\theta^2\right), \tag{4.4}$$

respectively, where subscript h indicates a heuristic trader and m is the representativeness heuristic parameter and $m > 1$. Note from Eqs. (4.3) and (4.4) that if the representativeness heuristic parameter is one, then heuristic traders become indistinguishable from rational traders[3].

Using Eqs. (4.1), (4.2), (4.3), and (4.4), the equations for $E_h(\theta\,|S)$ and $Var_h(\theta\,|S)$ are computed as:

$$E_h(\theta\,|S) = \overline{\theta} + \frac{m\sigma_\theta^2}{\sigma_\theta^2 + \sigma_\epsilon^2}\left(S - \overline{\theta}\right), \tag{4.5}$$

and

$$Var_h(\theta\,|S) = \sigma_\theta^2 - \frac{m\sigma_\theta^4}{\sigma_\theta^2 + \sigma_\epsilon^2}, \tag{4.6}$$

respectively. To ensure that $Var_h(\theta\,|S)$ is positive, the representativeness heuristic parameter must satisfy:

$$1 < m < \frac{\sigma_\theta^2 + \sigma_\epsilon^2}{\sigma_\theta^2}. \tag{4.7}$$

---

[1] The derivations of Eqs. (4.1) and (4.2) use the fact that the random variables θ and ϵ are independently and normally distributed.

[2] The representativeness heuristic is also referred to as the base-rate underweighting. The base-rate underweighting is described in Kahneman and Tversky (1973), Tversky and Kahneman (1974), and Grether (1980).

[3] Eq. (4.3) modeling heuristic traders' conditional mean of the asset payoff is the same as in the paper of Fischer and Verrecchia (1999).

In addition, note from Eqs. (4.1) and (4.5) that if the informational signal is greater than the expected payoff of the asset, then a heuristic trader has a larger conditional mean of the asset payoff than a rational trader does; also, if the informational signal is smaller than the expected payoff of the asset, then a heuristic trader has a smaller conditional mean of the asset payoff than a rational trader does. In addition, Eqs. (4.2) and (4.6) suggest that for any given informational signal, a heuristic trader has a smaller conditional variance of the asset payoff than a rational trader does.

Both rational and heuristic traders have an exponential utility function. In other words, for $i = r, h, U(w_i) = -e^{-aw_i}$, where a is the coefficient of absolute risk aversion and $a > 0$, and w_i is trader $i's$ wealth. Trader $i's$ wealth is the summation of his initial wealth (denoted as w) and the gain or loss derived from trading the assets. Since the payoff of the risk-free asset is one, it follows that the price of the risky-free asset is one. Hence, there is no gain or loss from trading the risk-free asset. Denote p as the asset price and X_i, where $i = r, h$, as trader $i's$ demand for the asset. Hence, for $i = r, h$, $w_i = w + X_i(\theta - p)$. In the competitive securities market, each trader takes the asset price as given. Due to the fact that the variables θ and ϵ are independently and normally distributed, trader $i's$ demand for the asset maximizing his exponential utility can be solved from: for $i = r, h$,

$$\max_{X_i} E_i(w_i\,|S) - \frac{a}{2} Var_i(w_i\,|S),$$

$$s.t.\ w_i = w + X_i(\theta - p). \tag{4.8}$$

Specifically, with Eqs. (4.1), (4.2), (4.5), and (4.6), the optimization problem (4.8) is solved to generate the demand functions for rational and heuristic traders as:

$$X_r = \frac{\overline{\theta} + \eta\left(S - \overline{\theta}\right) - p}{a\sigma_\theta^2(1-\eta)}, \tag{4.9}$$

and

$$X_h = \frac{\overline{\theta} + m\eta\left(S - \overline{\theta}\right) - p}{a\sigma_\theta^2(1-m\eta)}, \tag{4.10}$$

respectively, where $\eta = \frac{\sigma_\theta^2}{\sigma_\theta^2+\sigma_\epsilon^2} < 1$.

The total supply of the asset in the market is assumed to be zero. Hence, the market-clearing condition that equals the total demand for the asset to the total supply of the asset is described by:

$$\lambda X_r + (1-\lambda)X_h + x = 0, \tag{4.11}$$

where λ denotes the proportion of rational traders in the population consisting of rational and heuristic traders.

Note that noise traders are considered as net buyers of the asset if noise traders' demand for the asset is positive; otherwise, noise traders are considered as net sellers of the asset.

In addition, substituting Eqs. (4.9) and (4.10) into Eq. (4.11) results in the asset price as[4]:

$$p = \frac{-\left(\overline{\theta} + ax\sigma_\theta^2\right)(1-\eta)(1-m\eta) + S\eta\left[m(\eta-1) - \lambda(1-m)\right]}{\eta - 1 + \lambda\eta(m-1)}. \tag{4.12}$$

Also, substituting Eq. (4.12) into Eq. (4.9) gives rise to the demand function for heuristic traders as:

$$X_r = \frac{-1}{a\sigma_\theta^2\left(\eta - 1 + \lambda\eta(m-1)\right)}\left(ax\sigma_\theta^2(m\eta - 1) - \eta(m-1)(1-\lambda)\left(S - \overline{\theta}\right)\right). \tag{4.13}$$

Similarly, substituting Eq. (4.12) into Eq. (4.10) results in the demand function for heuristic traders as[5]:

$$X_h = \frac{1}{a\sigma_\theta^2\left(\eta - 1 + \lambda\eta(m-1)\right)}\left(ax\sigma_\theta^2(1-\eta) - \lambda\eta(m-1)\left(S - \overline{\theta}\right)\right). \tag{4.14}$$

4.3 The Results

This section analyzes how the representativeness heuristic causes the asset price to overreact or underreact to good news or bad news in the case of noise traders being net buyers or sellers of the asset.

Before the analysis, the definitions needed for the analysis are first specified below:

The asset price overreaction to an informational signal occurs if in response to the informational signal, rational traders buy (sell) the asset and at the same time, the asset price is higher (lower) than what it would be in the market with rational traders and noise traders. On the other hand, the asset price underreaction to an informational signal occurs if in responding to the informational signal, rational traders buy (sell) the asset and at the same time, the asset price is not as high (low) as it would be in the market with rational traders and noise traders.

In addition, the definitions of good news and bad news are as follows. An informational signal is considered as bad news if the signal is smaller than the expected payoff of the asset; otherwise, the informational signal is considered as good news. Furthermore, according to how far the informational signal is greater than the expected payoff of the asset, the good news is further classified as slightly good news if $\overline{\theta} \leq S < \overline{\theta} + a\,|x|\,\sigma_\theta^2$, very good news if $\overline{\theta} + a\,|x|\,\sigma_\theta^2 \leq S < \overline{\theta} + \frac{a|x|\sigma_\theta^2(1-m\eta)}{\eta(m-1)(1-\lambda)}$, where $\frac{1-m\eta}{\eta(m-1)(1-\lambda)} > 1$, and extremely good news if $S \geq \overline{\theta} + \frac{a|x|\sigma_\theta^2(1-m\eta)}{\eta(m-1)(1-\lambda)}$. Similarly, based on how far the informational signal is smaller than the expected payoff of the

[4] Note from Eq. (4.12) that $E(p) = \overline{\theta}$.

[5] Note from Eqs. (4.13) and (4.14) that $E(X_i) = 0$ for $i = r, h$.

asset, bad news is further classified as slightly bad news if $\overline{\theta} - a\,|x|\,\sigma_\theta^2 < S < \overline{\theta}$, very bad news if $\overline{\theta} - \frac{a|x|\sigma_\theta^2(1-m\eta)}{\eta(m-1)(1-\lambda)} < S \le \overline{\theta} - a\,|x|\,\sigma_\theta^2$, and extremely bad news if $S \le \overline{\theta} - \frac{a|x|\sigma_\theta^2(1-m\eta)}{\eta(m-1)(1-\lambda)}$.

In addition, to analyze whether the asset price is greater than $E_r\,(\theta\,|S)$, the equation for $p - E_r\,(\theta\,|S)$ is computed from Eqs. (4.1) and (4.12) as:

$$p - E_r\,(\theta\,|S) = \frac{1-\eta}{\eta - 1 + \lambda\eta(m-1)}\left(ax\sigma_\theta^2\,(m\eta - 1) - \eta(m-1)(1-\lambda)(S-\overline{\theta})\right). \tag{4.15}$$

Also, to analyze whether the asset price is greater than $E_h\,(\theta\,|S)$, the equation for $p - E_h\,(\theta\,|S)$ is computed from Eqs. (4.5) and (4.12) as:

$$p - E_h\,(\theta\,|S) = \frac{m\eta-1}{\eta - 1 + \lambda\eta(m-1)}\left(ax\sigma_\theta^2\,(1-\eta) - \lambda\eta(m-1)(S-\overline{\theta})\right). \tag{4.16}$$

In addition, to see whether heuristic traders' positions in the asset are larger than rational traders' in the case of heuristic traders taking trading positions on the same side as rational traders, the equation for $X_r - X_h$ is computed from Eqs. (4.13) and (4.14) as:

$$X_r - X_h = \eta(m-1)\frac{S - \overline{\theta} - ax\sigma_\theta^2}{a\sigma_\theta^2\,(\eta - 1 + \lambda\eta(m-1))}. \tag{4.17}$$

The remaining discussions of this section are classified into four scenarios. The four scenarios are distinguished according to whether the informational signal suggests good news or bad news and whether noise traders are net buyers or sellers of the asset. In each scenario, detailed analysis is provided on how the representativeness heuristic causes the asset price to overreact or underreact to good news or bad news. The following begins with the analysis in scenario (a).

Scenario (a): Informational signal indicates good news and noise traders are net sellers of the asset

Since $x < 0$ and $m < \frac{1}{\eta}$, it follows that $p > E_r\,(\theta\,|S)$ for $S > \overline{\theta} - \frac{ax\sigma_\theta^2(1-m\eta)}{\eta(m-1)(1-\lambda)}$ (see Eq. (4.15)). In addition, the inequality of $p > E_r\,(\theta\,|S)$, together with Eq. (4.9), implies that rational traders sell the asset in response to the good news. Also, since $x < 0$ and $m < \frac{1}{\eta}$, it follows that $p < E_h\,(\theta\,|S)$ (see Eq. (4.16)). In addition, the inequality of $p < E_h\,(\theta\,|S)$, together with (4.10), implies that heuristic traders buy the asset in response to the good news. Note that heuristic traders take trading positions opposite to rational traders. Hence, the asset price is not as low as it would be in the market with rational traders and noise traders. Thus, the asset price underreacts to the good news with $S > \overline{\theta} - \frac{ax\sigma_\theta^2(1-m\eta)}{\eta(m-1)(1-\lambda)}$.

In addition, with $x < 0$ and $m < \frac{1}{\eta}$, $p < E_r\,(\theta\,|S)$ for $\overline{\theta} \le S < \overline{\theta} - \frac{ax\sigma_\theta^2(1-m\eta)}{\eta(m-1)(1-\lambda)}$ (see Eq. (4.15)). Also, the inequality of $p < E_r\,(\theta\,|S)$, together with Eq. (4.9), implies that rational traders buy the asset in response to the good news. Note that

$X_r < X_h$ (see Eq. (4.17)). Hence, heuristic traders take larger positions in buying the asset than rational traders. As a result, the asset price is higher than what it would be in the market with rational traders and noise traders. That is, the asset price overreacts to the good news with $\overline{\theta} \leq S < \overline{\theta} - \frac{ax\sigma_\theta^2(1-m\eta)}{\eta(m-1)(1-\lambda)}$.

The results in scenario (a) are presented in Proposition 1 below:

Proposition 1 *With noise traders being net sellers of the asset, the asset price underreacts to the good news with* $S > \overline{\theta} - \frac{ax\sigma_\theta^2(1-m\eta)}{\eta(m-1)(1-\lambda)}$ *and overreacts to the good news with* $\overline{\theta} \leq S < \overline{\theta} - \frac{ax\sigma_\theta^2(1-m\eta)}{\eta(m-1)(1-\lambda)}$.

The results of Proposition 1, together with the definitions of the different types of good news, suggest that with noise traders being net sellers of the asset, the asset price underreacts to extremely good news and overreacts to slightly good news or very good news. The intuition behind these results is as follows. Note that with noise traders being net sellers of the asset, heuristic traders buy the asset in response to the good news. The reason for heuristic traders buying the asset is that in the case of the signal suggesting good news, a heuristic trader has a larger conditional mean of the asset payoff than a rational trader does. If the signal suggests extremely good news, then heuristic traders' positions in buying the asset are very large and the asset price is driven too high. Hence, rational traders profit from trading in a direction opposite to heuristic traders and the asset price is not as low as it would be in the market with rational traders and noise traders. Thus, the asset price underreacts to the extremely good news.

If the signal suggests very good news or slightly good news, then heuristic traders' positions in buying the asset are not as large as in the previous case in which the signal suggests extremely good news. Consequently, the asset price is not driven as high as in that case and rational traders profit from trading on the same side as heuristic traders. Note that in the case of the signal suggesting good news, a heuristic trader has a larger conditional mean of the asset payoff than a rational trader does. Hence, heuristic traders take larger positions in buying the asset than rational traders and the asset price is higher than what it would be in the market with rational traders and noise traders. That is, the asset price overreacts to very good news or slightly good news.

Scenario (b): Informational signal indicates good news and noise traders are net buyers of the asset

Note that $\frac{ax\sigma_\theta^2(1-\eta)}{\lambda\eta(m-1)} > ax\sigma_\theta^2 > 0$ (due to $x > 0$ and $m < \frac{1}{\eta}$). Hence, according to the realization of the signal, the discussions in scenario (b) are classified into three cases: case (a), where $S > \overline{\theta} + \frac{ax\sigma_\theta^2(1-\eta)}{\lambda\eta(m-1)}$; case (b), where $\overline{\theta} + ax\sigma_\theta^2 < S < \overline{\theta} + \frac{ax\sigma_\theta^2(1-\eta)}{\lambda\eta(m-1)}$; and case (c), where $\overline{\theta} \leq S < \overline{\theta} + ax\sigma_\theta^2$. In each case, detailed analysis is provided on how the representativeness heuristic causes the asset price to overreact or underreact to good news. The following begins with the analysis in case (a).

Case (a), where $S > \overline{\theta} + \frac{ax\sigma_\theta^2(1-\eta)}{\lambda\eta(m-1)}$: With this inequality, $p > E_r(\theta\,|S)$ (see Eq. (4.15)) and $p < E_h(\theta\,|S)$ (see Eq. (4.16)). In addition, the inequality of

$p > E_r(\theta\,|S)$, together with Eq. (4.9), implies that rational traders sell the asset in response to the good news. Also, the inequality of $p < E_h(\theta\,|S)$, together with Eq. (4.10), implies that heuristic traders buy the asset in response to the good news. Since heuristic traders take trading positions opposite to rational traders, it follows that the asset price is not as low as it would be in the market with rational traders and noise traders. Thus, the asset price underreacts to the good news with $S > \overline{\theta} + \frac{ax\sigma_\theta^2(1-\eta)}{\lambda\eta(m-1)}$.

Case (b), where $\overline{\theta} + ax\sigma_\theta^2 < S < \overline{\theta} + \frac{ax\sigma_\theta^2(1-\eta)}{\lambda\eta(m-1)}$: With these inequalities, $p > E_r(\theta\,|S)$ (see Eq. (4.15)) and $p > E_h(\theta\,|S)$ (see Eq. (4.16)). In addition, the inequality of $p > E_r(\theta\,|S)$, together with Eq. (4.9), implies that rational traders sell the asset in response to the good news. Also, the inequality of $p > E_h(\theta\,|S)$, together with Eq. (4.10), implies that heuristic traders sell the asset in response to the good news. In addition, since $X_r < X_h$ (see Eq. (4.17)), it follows that heuristic traders take smaller positions in selling the asset than rational traders. Hence, the asset price is not as low as it would be in the market with rational traders and noise traders. That is, the asset price underreacts to the good news with $\overline{\theta} + ax\sigma_\theta^2 < S < \overline{\theta} + \frac{ax\sigma_\theta^2(1-\eta)}{\lambda\eta(m-1)}$.

Case (c), where $\overline{\theta} \leq S < \overline{\theta} + ax\sigma_\theta^2$: With these inequalities, $p > E_r(\theta\,|S)$ (see Eq. (4.15)) and $p > E_h(\theta\,|S)$ (see Eq. (4.16)). In addition, the inequality of $p > E_r(\theta\,|S)$, together with Eq. (4.9), implies that rational traders sell the asset in response to the good news. Also, the inequality of $p > E_h(\theta\,|S)$, together with Eq. (4.10), implies that heuristic traders sell the asset in response to the good news. Note that $X_r > X_h$ (see Eq. (4.17)). Hence, heuristic traders take larger positions in selling the asset than rational traders. Therefore, the asset price is lower than what it would be in the market with rational traders and noise traders. Thus, the asset price overreacts to the good news with $\overline{\theta} \leq S < \overline{\theta} + ax\sigma_\theta^2$.

Proposition 2 below presents the results in scenario (b).

Proposition 2 *With noise traders being net buyers of the asset, the asset price underreacts to the good news with* $S > \overline{\theta} + ax\sigma_\theta^2$ *and overreacts to the good news with* $\overline{\theta} \leq S < \overline{\theta} + ax\sigma_\theta^2$.

Note from the results of Proposition 2 that in the case of noise traders being net buyers of the asset, the asset price underreacts to extremely good news or very good news and overreacts to slightly good news. The intuition behind these results is as follows. Note that in the case of noise traders being net buyers of the asset, rational traders sell the asset in response to the good news. The reason for rational traders selling the asset is that in the case of the signal suggesting good news, a rational trader has a smaller conditional mean of the asset payoff than a heuristic trader does. If the signal suggests extremely good news, then rational traders' positions in selling the asset are very large and the asset price is driven too low. Hence, heuristic traders profit from trading in a direction opposite to rational traders and the asset price is not as low as it would be in the market with rational traders and noise traders. That is, the asset price underreacts to the extremely good news.

If the signal suggests very good news, then rational traders' positions in selling the asset are not as large as in the previous case in which the signal suggests extremely good news. Hence, the asset price is not driven as low as in that case and heuristic traders profit from trading on the same side as rational traders. In addition, since with the signal suggesting good news, a heuristic trader has a larger conditional mean of the asset payoff than a rational trader does, it follows that heuristic traders take smaller positions in selling the asset than rational traders. As a result, the asset price is not as low as it would in the market with rational traders and noise traders. Thus, the asset price underreacts to the very good news.

In addition, if the signal suggests slightly good news, then rational traders' positions in selling the asset are not as large as in the previous case in which the signal suggests extremely good news. Hence, the asset price is not driven as low as in that case. Consequently, heuristic traders profit from trading on the same side as rational traders. Note that for any given signal, a heuristic trader has a smaller conditional variance of the asset payoff than a rational trader does. Hence, heuristic traders take larger positions in selling the asset than rational traders and the asset price is lower than what it would in the market with rational traders and noise traders. That is, the asset price overreacts to the slightly good news.

Scenario (c): Informational signal indicates bad news and noise traders are net sellers of the asset

Note that $\frac{ax\sigma_\theta^2(1-\eta)}{\lambda\eta(m-1)} < ax\sigma_\theta^2 < 0$ (due to $x < 0$ and $m < \frac{1}{\eta}$). Hence, according to the realization of the signal, the discussions in scenario (c) are classified into three cases: case (a), where $S < \overline{\theta} + \frac{ax\sigma_\theta^2(1-\eta)}{\lambda\eta(m-1)}$; case (b), where $\overline{\theta} + \frac{ax\sigma_\theta^2(1-\eta)}{\lambda\eta(m-1)} < S < \overline{\theta} + ax\sigma_\theta^2$; and case (c), where $\overline{\theta} > S > \overline{\theta} + ax\sigma_\theta^2$. Detailed analysis is provided for each case on how the representativeness heuristic causes the asset price to overreact or underreact to the bad news. The following begins with the analysis in case (a).

Case (a), where $S < \overline{\theta} + \frac{ax\sigma_\theta^2(1-\eta)}{\lambda\eta(m-1)}$: Due to this inequality, $p < E_r(\theta\,|S)$ (see Eq. (4.15)) and $p > E_h(\theta\,|S)$ (see Eq. (4.16)). In addition, the inequality of $p < E_r(\theta\,|S)$, together with Eq. (4.9), implies that rational traders buy the asset in response to the bad news. Also, the inequality of $p > E_h(\theta\,|S)$, together with Eq. (4.10), implies that heuristic traders sell the asset in response to the bad news. In addition, since heuristic traders take trading positions opposite to rational traders, it follows that the asset price is not as high as it would be in the market with rational traders and noise traders. Thus, the asset price underreacts to the bad news with $S < \overline{\theta} + \frac{ax\sigma_\theta^2(1-\eta)}{\lambda\eta(m-1)}$.

Case (b), where $\overline{\theta} + \frac{ax\sigma_\theta^2(1-\eta)}{\lambda\eta(m-1)} < S < \overline{\theta} + ax\sigma_\theta^2$: Because of these inequalities, $p < E_r(\theta\,|S)$ (see Eq. (4.15)) and $p < E_h(\theta\,|S)$ (see Eq. (4.16)). In addition, the inequality of $p < E_r(\theta\,|S)$, together with Eq. (4.9), implies that rational traders buy the asset in response to the bad news. Also, the inequality of $p < E_h(\theta\,|S)$, together with Eq. (4.10), implies that heuristic traders buy the asset in response to the bad news. Note that $X_r > X_h$ (see Eq. (4.17)). Hence, heuristic traders take smaller positions in buying the asset than rational traders. Therefore, the asset price is not as high as it would be in the market with rational traders and noise traders. That is, the asset price underreacts to the bad news with $\overline{\theta} + \frac{ax\sigma_\theta^2(1-\eta)}{\lambda\eta(m-1)} < S < \overline{\theta} + ax\sigma_\theta^2$.

Case (c), where $\overline{\theta} > S > \overline{\theta} + ax\sigma_\theta^2$: Due to these inequalities, $p < E_r(\theta\,|S)$ (see Eq. (4.15)) and $p < E_h(\theta\,|S)$ (see Eq. (4.16)). In addition, the inequality of $p < E_r(\theta\,|S)$, together with Eq. (4.9), implies that rational traders buy the asset in response to the bad news. Also, the inequality of $p < E_h(\theta\,|S)$, together with Eq. (4.10), implies that heuristic traders buy the asset in response to the bad news. In addition, since $X_r < X_h$ (see Eq. (4.17)), it follows that heuristic traders take larger positions in buying the asset than rational traders. Therefore, the asset price is higher than what it would be in the market with rational traders and noise traders. Thus, the asset price overreacts to the bad news with $\overline{\theta} + ax\sigma_\theta^2 < S < \overline{\theta}$.

The results in scenario (c) are contained in Proposition 3 below:

Proposition 3 *With noise traders being net sellers of the asset, the asset price underreacts to the bad news with* $S < \overline{\theta} + ax\sigma_\theta^2$ *and overreacts to the bad news with* $\overline{\theta} + ax\sigma_\theta^2 < S < \overline{\theta}$.

With the definitions of the different types of bad news, the results of Proposition 3 mean that in the case of noise traders being net sellers of the asset, the asset price underreacts to the extremely bad news or very bad news and overreacts to the slightly bad news. These results can be intuitively explained as follows. Note that in the case of noise traders being net sellers of the asset, rational traders buy the asset in response to the bad news. The reason for rational traders buying the asset is that with the signal suggesting bad news, a rational trader has a larger conditional mean of the asset payoff than a heuristic trader does. If the signal suggests extremely bad news, then rational traders' positions in buying the asset are very large and the asset price is driven too high. As a result, heuristic traders profit from trading in a direction opposite to rational traders. Hence, the asset price is not as high as it would be in the market with rational traders and noise traders. That is, the asset price underreacts to the extremely bad news.

If the signal suggests very bad news, then rational traders' positions in buying the asset are not as large as in the previous case in which the signals suggest extremely bad news. Consequently, the asset price is not driven as high as in that case and heuristic traders profit from trading on the same side as rational traders. In addition, since with the signal suggesting bad news, a heuristic trader has a smaller conditional mean of the asset payoff than a rational trader does, it follows that heuristic traders take smaller positions in buying the asset than rational traders. Hence, the asset price is not as high as it would be in the market with rational traders and noise traders. That is, the asset price underreacts to the very bad news.

In addition, if the signal suggests slightly bad news, then rational traders' positions in buying the asset are not as large as in the previous case in which the signal suggests extremely bad news. As a result, the asset price is not driven as high as in that case and heuristic traders profit from trading on the same side as rational traders. Note that a heuristic trader has a smaller conditional variance of the asset payoff than a rational trader does. Hence, heuristic traders take larger positions in buying the asset than rational traders and the asset price is higher than what it would be in the market with rational traders and noise traders. Thus, the asset price overreacts to the slightly bad news.

Scenario (d): Informational signal indicates bad news and noise traders are net buyers of the asset

Note that with $x > 0$ and $m < \frac{1}{\eta}$, $p > E_r(\theta\,|S)$ for $\overline{\theta} - \frac{ax\sigma_\theta^2(1-m\eta)}{\eta(m-1)(1-\lambda)} < S < \overline{\theta}$ (see Eq. (4.15)). In addition, the inequality of $p > E_r(\theta\,|S)$, together with Eq. (4.9), implies that rational traders sell the asset in responding to the bad news. Also, note that with $x > 0$ and $m < \frac{1}{\eta}$, $p > E_h(\theta\,|S)$ (see Eq. (4.16)). In addition, the inequality of $p > E_h(\theta\,|S)$, together with Eq. (4.10), implies that heuristic traders sell the asset in response to the bad news. Also, since $X_r > X_h$ (see Eq. (4.17)), it follows that heuristic traders take larger positions in selling the asset than rational traders. Hence, the asset price is lower than what it would be in the market with rational traders and noise traders. Thus, the asset price overreacts to the bad news with $\overline{\theta} - \frac{ax\sigma_\theta^2(1-m\eta)}{\eta(m-1)(1-\lambda)} < S < \overline{\theta}$.

In addition, note that with $x > 0$ and $m < \frac{1}{\eta}$, $p < E_r(\theta\,|S)$ for $S < \overline{\theta} - \frac{ax\sigma_\theta^2(1-m\eta)}{\eta(m-1)(1-\lambda)}$ (see Eq. (4.15)). Also, the inequality of $p < E_r(\theta\,|S)$, together with Eq. (4.9), implies that in response to the bad news, rational traders buy the asset. Note that with $x > 0$ and $m < \frac{1}{\eta}$, $p > E_h(\theta\,|S)$ (see Eq. (4.16)). Also, the inequality of $p > E_h(\theta\,|S)$, together with Eq. (4.10), implies that heuristic traders sell the asset in response to the bad news. Note that in response to the bad news, heuristic traders take trading positions opposite to rational traders. Hence, the asset price is not as high as it would be in the market with rational traders and noise traders. That is, the asset price underreacts to the bad news with $S < \overline{\theta} - \frac{ax\sigma_\theta^2(1-m\eta)}{\eta(m-1)(1-\lambda)}$.

Proposition 4 below states the results in scenario (d).

Proposition 4 *With noise traders being net buyers of the asset, the asset price underreacts to the bad news with* $S < \overline{\theta} - \frac{ax\sigma_\theta^2(1-m\eta)}{\eta(m-1)(1-\lambda)}$ *and overreacts to the bad news with* $\overline{\theta} > S > \overline{\theta} - \frac{ax\sigma_\theta^2(1-m\eta)}{\eta(m-1)(1-\lambda)}$.

The results of Proposition 4, together with the definitions of the different types of bad news, imply that in the case of noise traders being net buyers of the asset, the asset price overreacts to the slightly bad news or very bad news and underreacts to the extremely bad news. The intuitive story behind these results is explained as follows. Note that in the case of noise traders being net buyers of the asset, heuristic traders sell the asset in response to the bad news. The reason for heuristic traders selling the asset is that with the signal suggesting bad news, a heuristic trader has a smaller conditional mean of the asset payoff than a rational trader does. If the signal suggests extremely bad news, then heuristic traders' positions in selling the asset are very large. Hence, the asset price is driven too low and rational traders profit from trading in a direction to heuristic traders. Therefore, the asset price is not as high as it would be in the market with rational traders and noise traders. That is, the asset price underreacts to the extremely bad news.

In addition, if the signal suggests very bad news or slightly bad news, then heuristic traders' positions in selling the asset are not as large as in the previous case in which the signal suggests extremely bad news. As a result, the asset price is not driven as low as in that case and rational traders profit from trading on the same side as heuristic traders. Note that a heuristic trader has a smaller conditional variance of the asset payoff than a rational trader does. Hence, heuristic traders take larger positions in selling the asset than rational traders. Therefore, the asset price is lower than what it would be in the market with rational traders and noise traders. Thus, the asset price overreacts to the slightly bad news or very bad news.

4.4 Concluding Remarks

This chapter proves that the representativeness heuristic is capable of causing the asset price to overreact or underreact to the good news or bad news. Specifically, this chapter sets up a static model of a competitive securities market. In the market, there are two assets: risk-free asset and risky asset. The payoff of the risk-free asset is one and the payoff of the risky asset is normally distributed. In addition, there are three types of traders: rational traders, heuristic traders and noise traders. Noise traders' demand for the asset is assumed to be random. Before any trade takes place, rational and heuristic traders receive an informational signal about the asset payoff. Due to the representativeness heuristic, with the informational signal greater (smaller) than the expected payoff of the asset, a heuristic trader has a larger (smaller) conditional mean of the asset payoff than a rational trader does. In addition, for any given informational signal, a heuristic trader has a smaller conditional variance of the asset payoff than a rational trader does.

In the competitive securities market, the asset price overreaction to new information occurs if in response to the new information, heuristic traders' positions in the asset are in the same direction as rational traders' and bigger than rational traders'. In addition, the asset price underreaction to the new information occurs if in response to the new information, either heuristic traders' positions in the asset are in the same direction as rational traders' and smaller than rational traders' or in a direction opposite to rational traders'.

The results of this chapter suggest that regardless of noise traders being net buyers or sellers of the asset, the representativeness heuristic causes the asset price to overreact to slightly good news or slightly bad news and to underreact to extremely good news or extremely bad news; in addition, whether the representativeness heuristic causes the asset price to overreact or underreact to the very good news or very bad news depends on whether noise traders are net buyers or sellers of the asset.

Chapter 5
Representativeness Heuristic and Asset Price Overreaction or Underreaction to New Information in the Presence of Strategic Interaction

5.1 Introduction

This chapter examines how the representativeness heuristic causes the asset price to overreact or underreact to good news or bad news in the presence of strategic interaction. It proves that the representativeness heuristic is capable of causing the asset price overreaction or underreaction to good news or bad news.

These results are obtained in a static model of an asset market. In the market, there are three types of traders: rational traders, heuristic traders and noise traders. The asset payoff is unknown to all traders, but rational and heuristic traders receive an informational signal about the asset payoff before any trade takes place. Heuristic traders place too much weight on the current informational signal and not enough weight on their prior information when updating their beliefs about the asset payoff. Rational and heuristic traders are both risk-neutral. Noise traders trade for their liquidity needs. Hence, their demand for the asset is assumed to be random. There is one market maker in the market. The market maker supplies the liquidity to the market. The cost of doing so is assumed to be zero. To maximize their own expected profits, rational and heuristic traders strategically submit their market orders for the asset to the market maker. After observing the aggregate market orders for the asset of all traders, the market maker sets the asset price equal to the expected payoff of the asset conditional on the observed aggregate market orders for the asset of all traders.

In the equilibrium, the asset price depends on the proportion of heuristic traders, the representativeness heuristic parameter and the realization of the informational signal. This chapter proves that the representativeness heuristic is capable of causing the asset price to overreact or underreact to good news or bad news.

The reasons for the asset price to underreact or overreact to the good news are as follows. Note that the derivative of the asset price with respect to the proportion of heuristic traders can be broken down into two components. One component is the impact on the asset price of noise traders' demand for the asset, which is the derivative (with respect to the proportion of heuristic traders) of the multiplication of the pricing parameter and noise traders' demand for the asset. Note that the pricing parameter is the coefficient for both noise traders' demand for the asset and the aggregate demand for the asset of rational and heuristic traders in the asset pricing equation. The other

G. Y. Luo, *Asset Price Response to New Information*, SpringerBriefs in Finance, DOI 10.1007/978-1-4614-9369-3_5, © The Author(s) 2014

component is the impact on the asset price of the aggregate demand for the asset of rational and heuristic traders, which is defined as the derivative (with respect to the proportion of heuristic traders) of the multiplication of the pricing parameter and the aggregate demand for the asset of rational and heuristic traders. This impact is positive in the case of the signal suggesting good news. Hence, the net impact of these two components determines whether the derivative of the asset price with respect to the proportion of heuristic traders is positive or negative. If it is positive, then the asset price increases as the proportion of heuristic traders increases. In addition, assuming that rational traders buy the asset in response to the good news. Hence, with rational traders buying the asset in response to the good news, the positive sign of the derivative of the asset price with respect to the proportion of heuristic traders implies that the asset price is higher than what it would be in the market with rational traders and noise traders and the asset price overreacts to the good news. On the other hand, if the derivative of the asset price with respect to the proportion of heuristic traders is negative, then the asset price decreases as the proportion of heuristic traders increases. Hence, with rational traders buying the asset in response to the good news, the negative derivative of the asset price with respect to the proportion of heuristic traders implies that the asset price is not as high as it would be in the market with rational traders and noise traders and the asset price underreacts to the good news.

Similar explanations would apply to explaining why the asset price can underreact or overreact to bad news.

The remainder of this chapter consists of three sections. The next section describes the model. Section 3 presents the results. Section 4 concludes the chapter.

5.2 The Model

This section constructs a static model of an asset market allowing for strategic interaction among traders. In the market, there is one asset and one market maker. The market maker supplies liquidity to the market. The cost of doing so is assumed to be zero. There are rational and heuristic traders and noise traders in the market. Noise traders trade for their liquidity needs. Hence, their demand for the asset (denoted as x) is assumed to be normally distributed with the mean of zero and variance of σ_x^2. All traders submit their market orders for the asset to the market maker. The payoff of the asset is normally distributed with the mean of $\overline{\theta}$ and variance of σ_θ^2. Rational and heuristic traders receive an informational signal about the asset payoff before any trade occurs. The informational signal is modeled as: $S = \theta + \epsilon$ where ϵ is normally distributed with the mean of zero and variance of σ_ϵ^2. The random variables x, θ and ϵ are mutually independent. The informational signal is considered as good news if $S \geq \overline{\theta}$; otherwise, it is considered as bad news.

After receiving the informational signal about the asset payoff, rational traders update their conditional mean of the asset payoff according to:

$$E\left(\theta\,|(S,r)\right) = \overline{\theta} + \frac{\sigma_\theta^2}{\sigma_\theta^2 + \sigma_\epsilon^2}\left(S - \overline{\theta}\right), \tag{5.1}$$

where r indicates a rational trader. Note that Eq. (5.1) is derived by using the results of Theorem 1 in the appendix and the normality assumptions placed on the random variables ϵ and θ.

Heuristic traders exhibit representativeness heuristic. The representativeness heuristic is a type of behavioral bias. It is well-documented in psychologists' experiments (see Kahneman and Tversky 1973, Tversky and Kahneman 1974, and Grether 1980). In this model, traders with the representativeness heuristic place too much weight on current information and not enough weight on their prior knowledge when they update their beliefs about the asset payoff. Hence, heuristic traders' conditional mean of the asset payoff is modeled as:

$$E\left(\theta \,|(S,h)\right) = \overline{\theta} + m\left(E\left(\theta \,|(S,r)\right) - \overline{\theta}\right), \tag{5.2}$$

where h indicates a heuristic trader and m is the representativeness heuristic parameter and $m > 1$.

Substituting Eq. (5.1) into (5.2) results in:

$$E\left(\theta \,|(S,h)\right) = \overline{\theta} + \frac{m\sigma_\theta^2}{\sigma_\theta^2 + \sigma_\epsilon^2}\left(S - \overline{\theta}\right). \tag{5.3}$$

Note from Eq. (5.3) that if the informational signal is greater than the expected payoff of the asset, then a heuristic trader has a larger conditional mean of the asset payoff than a rational trader does; in addition, if the signal is smaller than the expected payoff of the asset, then a heuristic trader has a smaller conditional mean of the asset payoff than a rational trader does. Hence, heuristic traders overweight the new information and underweight their prior knowledge. This is consistent with the base rate underweighting or base rate fallacy characterized in Kahneman and Tversky (1973), Tversky and Kahneman (1974), and Grether (1980).[1]

Both rational and heuristic traders are considered as informed traders. It is assumed that there are N informed traders. The proportion of informed traders being heuristic traders is denoted as f, where $f \in (0, 1)$.

After receiving aggregate market orders for the asset of all traders, the market maker sets the asset price equal to the expected payoff of the asset conditional on the observed aggregate demand for the asset of all traders. Denote the asset price as P and the aggregate demand for the asset of all traders as D. Hence, the asset price is determined by:

$$P = E(\theta \,|D). \tag{5.4}$$

The equilibrium is characterized by: (a) Given the asset pricing rule (described in Eq. (5.4)), by taking into account the impact of his market order on the asset price and on the market orders for the asset of other traders, trader i, where $i \in \{1, 2, .., N\}$, of type j, $j = r, h$, chooses his market order for the asset (denoted as X_{ij}) to solve

$$\max_{X_{ij}} \left[E(\theta \,|(S, j)) - E(P|(S, X_{ij})\right] X_{ij}, \tag{5.5}$$

[1] The way that representativeness heuristic is modeled (i.e., Eq. (5.2)) is the same as in the paper of Fischer and Verrecchia (1999).

where $E(\theta\,|(S,j)) = E(\theta\,|(S,r))$ if $j = r$; $E(\theta\,|(S,j)) = E(\theta\,|(S,h))$ if $j = h$, and $E(P|(S,X_{ij})) = E(\theta|D)$. (b) Given the market orders for the asset of all traders, the market maker sets the asset price equal to the expected payoff of the asset conditional on the observed aggregate demand for the asset of all traders.

Note that rational and heuristic traders are risk-neutral in this model. Denote the total number of heuristic traders as N_h and the total number of rational traders as N_r. Hence, $N = N_r + N_h$. In addition, assume that the equilibrium market orders for the asset of rational and heuristic traders are linear functions of their informational signal. That is, for $i = 1, 2, .., N_r$,

$$X_{ir} = a_{ir} + b_{ir}S, \tag{5.6}$$

and for $i = 1, 2, .., N_h$,

$$X_{ih} = a_{ih} + b_{ih}S. \tag{5.7}$$

Also, assume that the equilibrium asset price follows the linear pricing rule:

$$P = \mu + \lambda D, \tag{5.8}$$

where $D = \sum_{i=1}^{N_r} X_{ir} + \sum_{i=1}^{N_h} X_{ih} + x$; and all the coefficients μ, λ; a_{ir} and b_{ir} for $i = 1, 2, .., N_r$; and a_{rh} and b_{ih} for $i = 1, 2, .., N_h$ are to be determined later.

In addition, substituting Eqs. (5.1), (5.3), (5.6), (5.7), and (5.8) into optimization problem (5.5) results in first-order conditions for optimization problem (5.5) as: for $\eta = \frac{\sigma_\theta^2}{\sigma_\theta^2 + \sigma_\epsilon^2}$,

$$\overline{\theta} + \eta\left(S - \overline{\theta}\right) - \mu - \lambda\left(2X_{ir} + \sum\nolimits_{\substack{n=1\\ n\neq i}}^{N_r} (a_{nr} + b_{nr}S) + \sum\nolimits_{n=1}^{N_h} (a_{nh} + b_{nh}S)\right) = 0, \tag{5.9}$$

and

$$\overline{\theta} + m\eta\left(S - \overline{\theta}\right) - \mu - \lambda\left(2X_{kh} + \sum\nolimits_{\substack{n=1\\ n\neq k}}^{N_h} (a_{nh} + b_{nh}S) + \sum\nolimits_{n=1}^{N_r} (a_{nr} + b_{nr}S)\right) = 0. \tag{5.10}$$

Also, substituting Eq. (5.6) into (5.9) and substituting Eq. (5.7) into (5.10) gives rise to:

$$a_{ij} = \frac{\overline{\theta} - \mu - R_j\eta\overline{\theta}}{\lambda} - A, \tag{5.11}$$

and

$$b_{ij} = \frac{R_j\eta}{\lambda} - B, \tag{5.12}$$

where $A = \sum_{n=1}^{N_r} a_{nr} + \sum_{n=1}^{N_h} a_{nh}$ and $B = \sum_{n=1}^{N_r} b_{nr} + \sum_{n=1}^{N_h} b_{nh}$.

Note from Eqs. (5.11) and (5.12), that for $i^{'} \neq i$, $a_{ij} = a_{i^{'}j}$ and $b_{ij} = b_{i^{'}j}$ for $j \in \{r, h\}$. Hence, denote $a_r = a_{ir}$ and $b_r = b_{ir}$ for $i = 1, 2, \ldots N_r$; denote $a_h = a_{ih}$ and $b_h = b_{ih}$ for $i = 1, 2, \ldots N_h$. Note that the coefficients a_r, a_h, b_r and b_h are computed from Eqs. (5.11) and (5.12) as:

$$a_r = \frac{\overline{\theta} - \mu + \eta\overline{\theta}(Nf(m-1) - 1)}{\lambda(N+1)}, \tag{5.13}$$

$$a_h = \frac{\overline{\theta} - \mu + \eta\overline{\theta}(N(1-f)(1-m) - m)}{\lambda(N+1)}, \tag{5.14}$$

$$b_r = \frac{\eta(1 + Nf(1-m))}{\lambda(N+1)}, \tag{5.15}$$

and

$$b_h = \frac{\eta(m - N(1-f)(1-m))}{\lambda(N+1)}, \tag{5.16}$$

respectively.

In addition, the asset price is computed from Eq. (5.4) as:

$$\begin{aligned} P &= E\left(\theta \,|A + BS + x = D\right) \\ &= \overline{\theta} + \frac{B\sigma_\theta^2}{B^2\sigma_S^2 + \sigma_x^2}(D - A - B\overline{\theta}). \end{aligned} \tag{5.17}$$

Also, Eqs. (5.8) and (5.17) imply that

$$\mu = \overline{\theta}, \tag{5.18}$$

and

$$\lambda^2 = \frac{N\eta\sigma_\theta^2(fm - f + 1)(Nf(1-m) + 1)}{\sigma_x^2(1+N)^2}. \tag{5.19}$$

Note that all traders of the same type have the same market orders for the asset. Hence, denote X_r as a rational trader's market order for the asset and X_h as a heuristic trader's market order for the asset. Therefore, from Eqs. (5.6), (5.7), (5.13) through (5.16), (5.17), and (5.18), the market orders for the asset of rational and heuristic traders and the asset price are computed as:

$$X_r = \frac{\eta(Nf - Nfm + 1)(S - \overline{\theta})}{\lambda(N+1)}, \tag{5.20}$$

$$X_h = \frac{\eta\,[N(1-f)(m-1)+m]\,(S-\overline{\theta})}{\lambda(N+1)}, \tag{5.21}$$

and

$$P = \overline{\theta} + \lambda x + \frac{N\eta(1-f+fm)(S-\overline{\theta})}{N+1}, \tag{5.22}$$

respectively, where the parameter λ is determined by Eq. (5.19).

Note from Eq. (5.19) that there is one positive solution and one negative solution for the parameter λ. The positive solution is chosen for the parameter λ to ensure that second-order conditions of optimization problem (5.5) hold and the asset price is an increasing function of the aggregate demand for the asset of all traders.

In addition, note from Eq. (5.20) that depending on the model parameters values, rational traders' demand for the asset, in response to the good news, can be positive or negative. Also, Eq. (5.21) implies that in response to the good news, heuristic traders' demand for the asset is positive. The reason for heuristic traders' demand for the asset being positive is that in the case of the signal suggesting good news, a heuristic trader has a larger conditional mean of the asset payoff than a rational trader does (due to the representativeness heuristic) (see Eqs. (5.1) and (5.3)). On the other hand, in the case of the signal suggesting bad news, a heuristic trader has a smaller conditional mean of the asset payoff than a rational trader (see Eqs. (5.1) and (5.3)). Hence, heuristic traders' demand for the asset is negative in response to the bad news (see Eq. (5.21)).

Also, the difference between the demand for the asset of heuristic traders and that of rational traders is computed from Eqs. (5.20) and (5.21) as:

$$X_h - X_r = \frac{(m-\eta+N\eta(m-1))\left(S-\overline{\theta}\right)}{\lambda\,(N+1)}. \tag{5.23}$$

Equation (5.23) suggests that heuristic traders' demand for the asset is larger than rational traders' in response to the good news, and it is smaller than rational traders' in response to the bad news. This is because, due to the representativeness heuristic, a heuristic trader has a larger conditional mean of the asset payoff than a rational trader does in the case of the signal suggesting good news; and also, in the case of the signal suggesting bad news, a heuristic trader has a smaller conditional mean of the asset payoff than a rational trader does (see Eqs. (5.1) and (5.3)).

5.3 The Results

This section presents detailed analysis on how the representativeness heuristic causes the asset price to overreact or underreact to the good news or bad news. Before the analysis, some definitions are first specified below:

In this model, the asset price overreaction to an informational signal occurs if in response to the informational signal, rational traders buy (sell) the asset and at the same time, the asset price is higher (lower) than what it would be in the market with rational traders and noise traders (i.e., $m = 1$, $f = 1$); on the other hand, the asset price underreaction to the informational signal occurs if in response to the informational signal, rational traders buy (sell) the asset and at the same time, the asset price is not as high (low) as it would be in the market with rational traders and noise traders (i.e., $m = 1$, $f = 1$).

To examine how the asset price changes as the proportion of heuristic traders changes, the derivative of the asset price with respect to the proportion of heuristic traders is computed from Eqs. (5.22) and (5.19) as:

$$\frac{dP}{df} = x\frac{d\lambda}{df} + \frac{N\eta(m-1)(S-\overline{\theta})}{N+1}, \tag{5.24}$$

where $\frac{d\lambda}{df} = \frac{N\eta\sigma_\theta^2(1-m)(N-2Nf+2Nfm-1)}{2\lambda(N+1)^2\sigma_x^2}$ (see Eq. (5.19)). Note from the equation of $\frac{d\lambda}{df}$ that $\frac{d\lambda}{df}$ is negative due to $m > 1$.

The following discusses four scenarios. These four scenarios are classified according to whether noise traders are net buyers or sellers of the asset and whether the informational signal indicates good news or bad news.

Scenario (a): the informational signal indicates good news and noise traders are net sellers of the asset

According to Eq. (5.24), if the signal indicates good news and noise traders are net sellers of the asset, then $\frac{dP}{df} > 0$ for $\overline{\theta} + \lambda x > 0$ (ensuring a positive asset price (see Eq. (5.22)). Note that the positive derivative of the asset price with respect to the proportion of heuristic traders indicates that the asset price is higher than what it would be in the market with rational traders and noise traders. In addition, note from Eq. (5.20) that if $Nf - Nfm + 1 > 0$ (or $f < \frac{1}{N(m-1)}$), then rational traders buy the asset in response to the good news. Hence, rational traders' buying the asset in response to the good news, together with the positive derivative of the asset price with respect to the proportion of heuristic traders, implies that the asset price overreacts to the good news. On the other hand, note from Eq. (5.20) that if $Nf - Nfm + 1 < 0$ (or $f > \frac{1}{N(m-1)}$) and $m > 1 + \frac{1}{N}$ (ensuring $f < 1$), then rational traders sell the asset in response to the good news. Hence, rational traders' selling the asset in response to the good news, together with the positive derivative of the asset price with respect to the proportion of heuristic traders, implies that the asset price is not as low as it would be in the market with rational traders and noise traders, and the asset price underreacts to the good news.

Scenario (b): the informational signal indicates bad news and noise traders are net buyers of the asset

Equation (5.24) suggests that if the signal indicates bad news and noise traders are net buyers of the asset, then $\frac{dP}{df} < 0$ for $\overline{\theta} > S > \overline{\theta} - \frac{(N+1)(\overline{\theta}+\lambda x)}{N\eta(1-f+fm)}$ (ensuring a positive asset price (see Eq. (5.22)). Also, note that for $Nf - Nfm + 1 > 0$ (or $f < \frac{1}{N(m-1)}$), rational traders sell the asset in response to the bad news (see Eq. (5.20)). Hence, rational traders' selling the asset in response to the bad news, together with the negative derivative of the asset price with respect to the proportion of heuristic traders, implies that the asset price is lower than what it would be in the market with rational traders and noise traders, and the asset price overreacts to the bad news.

In addition, Eq. (5.20) suggests that if $Nf - Nfm + 1 < 0$ (or $f > \frac{1}{N(m-1)}$) and $m > 1 + \frac{1}{N}$ (ensuring $f < 1$), then rational traders buy the asset in response to the bad news. Hence, rational traders' buying the asset in response to the bad news, together with the negative derivative of the asset price with respect to the proportion of heuristic traders, implies that the asset price is not as high as it would be in the market with rational traders and noise traders, and the asset price underreacts to the bad news.

Scenario (c): the informational signal indicates good news and noise traders are net buyers of the asset

According to Eq. (5.24), if the signal indicates good news with $S > \overline{\theta} + \frac{x\sigma_\theta^2(2Nf(m-1)+N-1)}{2\lambda(N+1)\sigma_x^2}$ and noise traders are net buyers of the asset, then $\frac{dP}{df} > 0$. Also, note from Eq. (5.20) that if $Nf - Nfm + 1 > 0$ (or $f < \frac{1}{N(m-1)}$), then rational traders buy the asset in response to the good news. Hence, rational traders' buying the asset in response to the good news, together with the positive derivative of the asset price with respect to the proportion of heuristic traders, implies that the asset price is higher than what it would be in the market with rational traders and noise traders, and the asset price overreacts to the good news with $S > \overline{\theta} + \frac{x\sigma_\theta^2(2Nf(m-1)+N-1)}{2\lambda(N+1)\sigma_x^2}$. On the other hand, note from Eq. (5.20) that if $Nf - Nfm + 1 < 0$ (or $f > \frac{1}{N(m-1)}$) and $m > 1 + \frac{1}{N}$ (ensuring $f < 1$), then rational traders sell the asset in response to the good news. Hence, rational traders' selling the asset in response to the good news, together with the positive derivative of the asset price with respect to the proportion of heuristic traders, implies that the asset price is not as low as it would be in the market with rational traders and noise traders, and the asset price underreacts to the good news with $S > \overline{\theta} + \frac{x\sigma_\theta^2(2Nf(m-1)+N-1)}{2\lambda(N+1)\sigma_x^2}$.

In addition, Eq. (5.24) also suggests that if the signal indicates good news with $\overline{\theta} < S < \overline{\theta} + \frac{x\sigma_\theta^2(2Nf(m-1)+N-1)}{2\lambda(N+1)\sigma_x^2}$ and noise traders are net buyers of the asset, then $\frac{dP}{df} < 0$. Also, note from Eq. (5.20) that if $Nf - Nfm + 1 > 0$ (or $f < \frac{1}{N(m-1)}$), then rational traders buy the asset in response to the good news. Hence, rational traders' buying the asset in response to the good news, together with the negative derivative of the asset price with respect to the proportion of heuristic traders, implies that the asset price is not as high as it would be in the market with rational traders and noise traders and the asset price underreacts to the good news with $\overline{\theta} < S < \overline{\theta} + \frac{x\sigma_\theta^2(2Nf(m-1)+N-1)}{2\lambda(N+1)\sigma_x^2}$. On the other hand, if $Nf - Nfm + 1 < 0$ (or $f > \frac{1}{N(m-1)}$) and $m > 1 + \frac{1}{N}$ (ensuring $f < 1$), then rational traders sell the asset in response to the good news (see Eq. (5.20)). Hence, rational traders' selling the asset in responding to the good news, together with the negative derivative of the asset price with respect to the proportion of heuristic traders, implies that the asset price is lower than what it would be in the market with rational traders and noise traders, and the asset price overreacts to the good news with $\overline{\theta} < S < \overline{\theta} + \frac{x\sigma_\theta^2(2Nf(m-1)+N-1)}{2\lambda(N+1)\sigma_x^2}$.

Scenario (d): the informational signal indicates bad news and noise traders are net sellers of the asset

Note from Eq. (5.24) that $\frac{dP}{df} > 0$ if noise traders are net sellers of the asset and the signal indicates bad news with $\overline{\theta} > S > \overline{\theta} + \frac{x\sigma_\theta^2(2Nf(m-1)+N-1)}{2\lambda(N+1)\sigma_x^2}$, where $\frac{x\sigma_\theta^2(2Nf(m-1)+N-1)}{2\lambda(N+1)\sigma_x^2} > -\frac{(N+1)(\overline{\theta}+\lambda x)}{N\eta(1-f+fm)}$ (ensuring a positive asset price (see Eq. (5.22))). Also, note from Eq. (5.20) that if $Nf - Nfm + 1 < 0$ (or $f > \frac{1}{N(m-1)}$) and $m > 1 + \frac{1}{N}$ (ensuring $f < 1$), then rational traders buy the asset in response to the bad news. Therefore, rational traders' buying the asset in response to the bad news, together with the positive derivative of the asset price with respect to the proportion of heuristic traders, implies that the asset price is higher than what it would be in the market with rational traders and noise traders, and the asset price overreacts to the bad news. In addition, note from Eq. (5.20) that if $Nf - Nfm + 1 > 0$ (or $f < \frac{1}{N(m-1)}$), then rational traders sell the asset in response to the bad news. Hence, rational traders' selling the asset in response to the bad news, together with the positive derivative of the asset price with respect to the proportion of heuristic traders, implies that the asset price is not as low as it would be in the market with rational traders and noise traders, and the asset price underreacts to the bad news.

In addition, note from Eq. (5.24) that $\frac{dP}{df} < 0$ if noise traders are net sellers of the asset and the signal indicates bad news with $\overline{\theta} - \frac{(N+1)(\overline{\theta}+\lambda x)}{N\eta(1-f+fm)} < S < \overline{\theta} + \frac{x\sigma_\theta^2(2Nf(m-1)+N-1)}{2\lambda(N+1)\sigma_x^2}$, where $-\frac{(N+1)(\overline{\theta}+\lambda x)}{N\eta(1-f+fm)} < \frac{x\sigma_\theta^2(2Nf(m-1)+N-1)}{2\lambda(N+1)\sigma_x^2}$ (ensuring a positive asset price (see Eq. (5.22))). Also, note from Eq. (5.20) that if $Nf - Nfm + 1 < 0$ (or $f > \frac{1}{N(m-1)}$) and $m > 1 + \frac{1}{N}$ (ensuring $f < 1$), then rational traders buy the asset in response to the bad news. Hence, rational traders' buying the asset in response to the bad news, together with the negative derivative of the asset price with respect to the proportion of heuristic traders, implies that the asset price is not as high as it would be in the market with rational traders and noise traders, and the asset price underreacts to the bad news. On the other hand, note from Eq. (5.20) that if $Nf - Nfm + 1 > 0$ (or $f < \frac{1}{N(m-1)}$), then rational traders sell the asset in response to the bad news. Hence, rational traders' selling the asset in response to the bad news, together with the negative derivative of the asset price with respect to the proportion of heuristic traders, implies that the asset price is lower than what it would be in the market with rational traders and noise traders, and the asset price overreacts to the bad news.

The results in scenarios (a), (b), (c), and (d) are summarized in two propositions below according to whether the informational signal indicates good news or bad news.

The following begins with proposition 1, stating the results from scenarios (a) and (c) on the asset price overreaction or underreaction to good news.

Proposition 1 (1) With noise traders being net sellers of the asset and $\overline{\theta} + \lambda x > 0$, if $f < \frac{1}{N(m-1)}$, then the asset price overreacts to the good news; on the other hand, if $f > \frac{1}{N(m-1)}$ and $m > 1 + \frac{1}{N}$ (ensuring $f < 1$), then the asset price underreacts to the good news. (2) With noise traders being net buyers of the asset and the informational signal indicating good news with $S > \overline{\theta} + \frac{x\sigma_\theta^2(2Nf(m-1)+N-1)}{2\lambda(N+1)\sigma_x^2}$, if $f < \frac{1}{N(m-1)}$, then the asset price overreacts to the good news; on the other hand, if $f > \frac{1}{N(m-1)}$ and $m > 1 + \frac{1}{N}$ (ensuring $f < 1$), then the asset price underreacts to the good news. (3) With noise traders being net buyers of the asset and the informational signal indicating good news with $\overline{\theta} < S < \overline{\theta} + \frac{x\sigma_\theta^2(2Nf(m-1)+N-1)}{2\lambda(N+1)\sigma_x^2}$, if $f < \frac{1}{N(m-1)}$, then the asset price underreacts to the good news; on the other hand, if $f > \frac{1}{N(m-1)}$ and $m > 1 + \frac{1}{N}$ (ensuring $f < 1$), then the asset price overreacts to the good news.

Proposition 2 below states the results from scenarios (b) and (d) on the asset price overreaction or underreaction to bad news.

Proposition 2 (1) With noise traders being net buyers of the asset and $\overline{\theta} > S > \overline{\theta} - \frac{(N+1)(\overline{\theta}+\lambda x)}{N\eta(1-f+fm)}$, if $f < \frac{1}{N(m-1)}$, then the asset price overreacts to the bad news; on the other hand, if $f > \frac{1}{N(m-1)}$ and $m > 1 + \frac{1}{N}$ (ensuring $f < 1$), then the asset price underreacts to the bad news. (2) With noise traders being net sellers of the asset and the signal indicating bad news with $\overline{\theta} > S > \overline{\theta} + \frac{x\sigma_\theta^2(2Nf(m-1)+N-1)}{2\lambda(N+1)\sigma_x^2}$, where $\frac{x\sigma_\theta^2(2Nf(m-1)+N-1)}{2\lambda(N+1)\sigma_x^2} > -\frac{(N+1)(\overline{\theta}+\lambda x)}{N\eta(1-f+fm)}$, if $f < \frac{1}{N(m-1)}$, then the asset price underreacts to the bad news; on the other hand, if $f > \frac{1}{N(m-1)}$ and $m > 1 + \frac{1}{N}$ (ensuring $f < 1$), then the asset price overreacts to the bad news. (3) With noise traders being net sellers of the asset and the signal indicating bad news with $\overline{\theta} - \frac{(N+1)(\overline{\theta}+\lambda x)}{N\eta(1-f+fm)} < S < \overline{\theta} + \frac{x\sigma_\theta^2(2Nf(m-1)+N-1)}{2\lambda(N+1)\sigma_x^2}$, where $-\frac{(N+1)(\overline{\theta}+\lambda x)}{N\eta(1-f+fm)} < \frac{x\sigma_\theta^2(2Nf(m-1)+N-1)}{2\lambda(N+1)\sigma_x^2}$, if $f < \frac{1}{N(m-1)}$, then the asset price overreacts to the bad news; on the other hand, if $f > \frac{1}{N(m-1)}$ and $m > 1 + \frac{1}{N}$ (ensuring $f < 1$), then the asset price underreacts to the bad news.

The results of propositions 1 and 2 suggest that the representativeness heuristic is capable of causing the asset price to underreact or overreact to the good news or bad news. The next section presents some concluding remarks.

5.4 Concluding Remarks

This chapter constructs a static model of an asset market. The payoff of the asset is unknown. But rational and heuristic traders receive an informational signal about the asset payoff before any trade takes place. Due to the representativeness heuristic, if the informational signal is greater than the expected payoff of the asset, then a heuristic trader has a larger conditional mean of the asset payoff than a rational trader does; in addition, if the signal is smaller than the expected payoff of the asset, then a heuristic trader has a smaller conditional mean of the asset payoff than a rational trader does. In the asset market, there is one market maker. The market maker supplies liquidity to the market. The cost of doing so is assumed to be zero. Rational and heuristic traders strategically submit their market orders for the asset to the market maker to maximize their own expected profits. After observing the aggregate demand for the asset of all traders, the market maker sets the asset price equal to the expected payoff of the asset conditional on the observed aggregate demand for the asset of all traders.

The equilibrium notion in the model is essentially the Nash equilibrium. This chapter finds that in the equilibrium, the asset price depends on the proportion of heuristic traders, the degree of the representativeness heuristic, and the realization of the informational signal. This chapter proves that representativeness heuristic is capable of causing the asset price to overreact or underreact to the good news or bad news.

Chapter 6
The Presence of Representativeness Heuristic and Conservatism Bias in an Asset Market

6.1 Introduction

The models in Chaps. 2–5 prove analytically that either conservatism or representativeness is capable of generating asset price overreaction or underreaction to good news or bad news.

This chapter extends the model of Kyle (1985) and attempts to explain the phenomena of asset price overreaction or underreaction to new information by using psychological biases, namely conservatism and representativeness heuristic. This chapter views conservatism and representativeness as two popular types of psychological biases among traders. For example, the strategies of technical traders' extrapolation based on the past patterns are popularly used among traders and they are examples of representativeness heuristic. Also, a lot of other strategies used by traders resemble the characteristics of conservatism.

Hence, this chapter sets up a static model of an asset market with one asset and one market maker. The payoff for the asset is unknown but all traders (rational, conservatism and heuristic traders) receive an informational signal about the asset payoff before any trade takes place.

Conservatism traders exhibit conservatism bias. The conservatism bias is a type of psychological bias well-documented in psychologists' experiments. Conservatism traders are slow to update their beliefs about the mean and variance of the asset payoff. As a result, if the informational signal is larger (smaller) than the expected payoff of the asset, then a conservatism trader has a smaller (larger) conditional mean of the asset payoff than a rational trader does. Heuristic traders exhibit representativeness heuristic. The representativeness heuristic is another type of psychological bias identified in psychologists' experiments. Heuristic traders with the representativeness place too much weight on current information and too little weight on their prior knowledge. Consequently, if the informational signal is greater (smaller) than the expected payoff of the asset, then a heuristic trader has a larger (smaller) conditional mean of the asset payoff than a rational trader does.

All traders submit their market orders for the asset strategically to the market maker to maximize their own expected profits. The market maker sets the asset price equal to the expected payoff of the asset conditional on the observed aggregate demand for the asset of all traders.

G. Y. Luo, *Asset Price Response to New Information*, SpringerBriefs in Finance,
DOI 10.1007/978-1-4614-9369-3_6, © The Author(s) 2014

The equilibrium in the asset market is essentially a Nash equilibrium. In the equilibrium, whether the asset price overreacts or underreacts to new information depends on the proportion of conservatism traders, the proportion of heuristic traders, the degree of conservatism bias, the degree of representativeness heuristic and the number of traders in the market. Define the total representativeness heuristic in the market as the total number of traders multiplying the proportion of heuristic traders and multiplying the degree of representativeness heuristic. Similarly, define the total conservatism bias in the market as the total number of traders multiplying the proportion of conservatism traders and multiplying the degree of conservatism bias. Hence, the results of the chapter can be stated as follows. The asset price overreacts to good news and bad news if the total representativeness heuristic minus the total conservatism bias in the market is greater than zero but less than one; otherwise, the asset price underreacts to good news and bad news.

The reasons behind the results are as follows. Note that if the total representativeness heuristic minus the total conservatism bias in the market is less than one, then rational traders buy the asset in response to the good news. Also, note that if the total representativeness heuristic is greater than the total conservatism bias in the market, then in the presence of good news, the impact on the asset price coming from heuristic traders dominates that coming from conservatism traders in the market. In addition, since a heuristic trader has a larger conditional mean of the asset payoff than a rational trader does in the case of the signal indicating good news (due to representativeness heuristic), it follows that the asset price is higher than what it would in the market with only rational traders. Hence, the asset price overreacts to the good news if the total representativeness heuristic minus the total conservatism bias in the market is greater than zero but less than one.

On the other hand, if the total conservatism bias is greater than the total representativeness heuristic in the market, then in the presence of good news, the impact on the asset price coming from conservatism traders dominates that coming from heuristic traders in the market. In addition, note that if the signal indicates good news, then a conservatism trader has a smaller conditional mean of the asset payoff than a rational trader does (due to the conservatism bias). Hence, the asset price is not as high as it would be in the market with only rational traders. Thus, with the total conservatism bias greater than the total representativeness heuristic in the market, asset price underreaction to the good news occurs.

However, if the total representativeness heuristic minus the total conservatism bias in the market is greater than one, then in response to the good news, rational traders sell the asset and also, the impact on the asset price coming from heuristic traders dominates that coming from conservatism traders. Note that if the signal indicates good news, then a heuristic trader has a larger conditional mean of the asset payoff than a rational trader does. Hence, the asset price is not as low as it would in the market with only rational traders. That is, the asset price underreacts to the good news if the total representativeness heuristic minus the total conservatism bias in the market is greater than one.

Similar intuitions to the above can be applied to explain the results of the asset price overreaction or underreaction to bad news.

The remainder of this chapter consists of three sections. The next section presents the model. The analysis and the results are in Sect. 3. Section 4 concludes the chapter.

6.2 The Model

Consider a static model of an asset market with one asset and one market maker. The market maker supplies liquidity to the market. The cost of doing so is assumed to be zero. All traders submit their market orders for the asset to the market maker. The payoff of the asset is normally distributed with the mean of $\overline{\theta}$ and variance of σ_{θ}^{2}. No trader knows the payoff of the asset; however, all traders receive an informational signal about the asset payoff before any trade occurs. The informational signal is modeled as: $S = \theta + \epsilon$ where ϵ is normally distributed with the mean of zero and variance of σ_{ϵ}^{2}. The random variables θ and ϵ are independent. The informational signal is considered as good news if $S \geq \overline{\theta}$; otherwise, it is considered as bad news.

There are three types of traders: rational traders, conservatism traders, and heuristic traders. After receiving the informational signal about the asset payoff, rational traders update their beliefs about the asset payoff according to:

$$E\left(\theta \mid (S,r)\right) = \overline{\theta} + \eta\left(S - \overline{\theta}\right), \tag{6.1}$$

where r indicates a rational trader and $\eta = \frac{\sigma_{\theta}^{2}}{\sigma_{\theta}^{2}+\sigma_{\epsilon}^{2}}$. Due to the normality assumptions placed on the random variables θ and ϵ, Eq. (6.1) follows from the results of Theorem 1 in the appendix.

Conservatism traders exhibit conservatism bias. The conservatism bias is a type of behavioral bias identified in psychologists' experiments (see Edwards 1968). Traders with the conservatism bias are slow to update their beliefs about the asset payoff relative to rational traders. Hence, conservatism traders' conditional mean for the asset payoff is modeled as:

$$E\left(\theta \mid (S,c)\right) = \overline{\theta} + m_c\left(E\left(\theta \mid (S,r)\right) - \overline{\theta}\right). \tag{6.2}$$

where the parameter c indicates a conservatism trader and $m_c \in (0,1)$. If the parameter m_c equals one, then conservatism traders become indistinguishable from rational traders. The degree of conservatism bias is measured by $1 - m_c$. Hence, the lower the parameter m_c, the greater is the traders' conservatism bias.

Substituting Eq. (6.1) into Eq. (6.2) results in:

$$E\left(\theta \mid (S,c)\right) = \overline{\theta} + m_c\eta\left(S - \overline{\theta}\right). \tag{6.3}$$

Note from Eq. (6.3) that if the signal is greater than the expected payoff of the asset, then a conservatism trader has a smaller conditional mean of the asset payoff than a rational trader does; in addition, if the signal is smaller than the expected payoff of the asset, then a conservatism trader has a larger conditional mean of the asset payoff than a rational trader does.

Heuristic traders exhibit representativeness heuristic. The representativeness heuristic is a type of behavioral bias. It is well-documented in psychologists' experiments (see Kahneman and Tversky 1973; Tversky and Kahneman (1974); Grether 1980). Traders with the representativeness heuristic place too much weight on current information and too little weight on their prior knowledge when they update their beliefs about the asset payoff. Hence, heuristic traders' conditional mean of the asset payoff is modeled as:

$$E\left(\theta \left|(S,h)\right.\right) = \overline{\theta} + m_h\left(E\left(\theta \left|(S,r)\right.\right) - \overline{\theta}\right), \tag{6.4}$$

where h indicates a heuristic trader and $m_h > 1$. If the parameter m_h equals one, then heuristic traders become indistinguishable from rational traders. The degree of representativeness is measured by $m_h - 1$. Hence, the higher above one the parameter m_h, the greater degree of representativeness heuristic.

Substituting Eq. (6.1) into (6.4) gives rise to:

$$E\left(\theta \left|(S,h)\right.\right) = \overline{\theta} + m_h\eta\left(S - \overline{\theta}\right). \tag{6.5}$$

Equation (6.5) suggests that if the informational signal is greater than the expected payoff of the asset, then a heuristic trader has a larger conditional mean of the asset payoff than a rational trader does; in addition, if the informational signal is smaller than the expected payoff of the asset, then a heuristic trader has a smaller conditional mean of the asset payoff than a rational trader does.

There are N traders in the market. Denote the proportion of traders being conservatism traders and heuristic traders as f_c and f_h, respectively, where $f_c \in (0, 1)$ and $f_h \in (0, 1)$.

After receiving the aggregate demand for the asset of all traders, the market maker sets the asset price equal to the expected payoff of the asset conditional on the observed aggregate demand for the asset of all traders. Denote the asset price as P and the aggregate demand as D. Hence, the asset price is determined by:

$$P = E(\theta \left|D\right.). \tag{6.6}$$

The equilibrium of the model is characterized by: (a) Given the asset pricing rule (stated in Eq. (6.6)), by taking into account the impact of his market order on the asset price and on the market orders for the asset of all other traders, trader i, where $i \in \{1, 2, .., N\}$, of type j, where $j \in \{r, c, h\}$, chooses his market order (denoted as X_{ij}) to solve:

$$\max_{X_{ij}} \left[E(\theta \left|(S,j)\right.) - E\left(P\left|\left(S,X_{ij}\right)\right.\right)\right] X_{ij}, \tag{6.7}$$

where $E(\theta \left|(S, j)\right.) = E(\theta \left|(S, r)\right.)$ if $j = r$; $E(\theta \left|(S, j)\right.) = E(\theta \left|(S, c)\right.)$ if $j = c$; $E(\theta \left|(S, j)\right.) = E(\theta \left|(S, h)\right.)$ if $j = h$; and $E(P|(S, X_{ij})) = E(\theta \left|D\right.)$. (b) Given the market orders for the asset of all traders, the market maker sets the asset price equal to the expected payoff of the asset conditional on the observed aggregate demand for the asset of all traders (see Eq. (6.6)).

Denote the total number of rational, conservatism, and heuristic traders as N_r, N_c and N_h, respectively. Hence, $N = N_r + N_h + N_c$. Note that rational, conservatism, and heuristic traders are risk-neutral. The equilibrium concept in the model is essentially a Nash equilibrium.

The following assumes that the equilibrium market orders for the asset of rational, conservatism, and heuristic traders are linear functions of their informational signal and the asset price is a linear function of the aggregate demand for the asset of all traders. Specifically, the equilibrium market orders for the asset of rational, conservatism, and heuristic traders are: for $i = 1, 2, .., N_r$,

$$X_{ir} = a_{ir} + b_{ir} S, \tag{6.8}$$

for $i = 1, 2, .., N_c$,

$$X_{ic} = a_{ic} + b_{ic} S, \tag{6.9}$$

and for $i = 1, 2, .., N_h$,

$$X_{ih} = a_{ih} + b_{ih} S. \tag{6.10}$$

Also, assume that the equilibrium asset price follows the linear pricing rule:

$$P = \mu + \lambda D, \tag{6.11}$$

where $D = \sum_{i=1}^{N_r} X_{ir} + \sum_{i=1}^{N_c} X_{ic} + \sum_{i=1}^{N_h} X_{ih}$; and all the coefficients μ, λ; a_{ir} and b_{ir} for ($i = 1, 2, .., N_r$); a_{rc}, and b_{ic} (for $i = 1, 2, .., N_c$); a_{rh}, and b_{ih} (for $i = 1, 2, .., N_h$) are to be determined later.

Substituting Eqs. (6.1), (6.3), (6.5) through (6.11) into optimization problem (6.7) results in the first-order conditions of optimization problem (6.7) as:

$$\begin{aligned}&\bar{\theta} + \eta\left(S - \bar{\theta}\right) - \mu - \lambda\Big(2X_{ir} + \sum\nolimits_{\substack{n=1\\ n\neq i}}^{N_r} (a_{nr} + b_{nr} S)\\ &\quad + \sum\nolimits_{n=1}^{N_h} (a_{nh} + b_{nh} S) + \sum\nolimits_{n=1}^{N_c} (a_{nc} + b_{nc} S)\Big) = 0,\end{aligned} \tag{6.12}$$

$$\begin{aligned}&\bar{\theta} + m_c\eta\left(S - \bar{\theta}\right) - \mu - \lambda\Big(2X_{kc} + \sum\nolimits_{\substack{n=1\\ n\neq k}}^{N_c} (a_{nc} + b_{nc} S)\\ &\quad + \sum\nolimits_{n=1}^{N_r} (a_{nr} + b_{nr} S) + \sum\nolimits_{n=1}^{N_h} (a_{nh} + b_{nh} S)\Big) = 0,\end{aligned} \tag{6.13}$$

and

$$\begin{aligned}&\bar{\theta} + m_h\eta\left(S - \bar{\theta}\right) - \mu - \lambda\Big(2X_{lh} + \sum\nolimits_{\substack{n=1\\ n\neq l}}^{N_h} (a_{nh} + b_{nh} S)\\ &\quad + \sum\nolimits_{n=1}^{N_r} (a_{nr} + b_{nr} S) + \sum\nolimits_{n=1}^{N_c} (a_{nc} + b_{nc} S)\Big) = 0.\end{aligned} \tag{6.14}$$

In addition, substituting Eqs. (6.8) through (6.10) into Eqs. (6.12), (6.13) and (6.14) gives rise to:

$$a_{ij} = \frac{\overline{\theta} - \mu - m_j \eta \overline{\theta}}{\lambda} - A, \tag{6.15}$$

and

$$b_{ij} = \frac{m_j \eta}{\lambda} - B, \tag{6.16}$$

where $A = \sum_{n=1}^{N_r} a_{nr} + \sum_{n=1}^{Nc} a_{nc} + \sum_{n=1}^{N_h} a_{nh}$; $B = \sum_{n=1}^{N_r} b_{nr} + \sum_{n=1}^{N_c} b_{nc} + \sum_{n=1}^{N_h} b_{nh}$; $m_j = 1$ if $j = r$; $m_j = m_c$ if $j = c$; and $m_j = m_h$ if $j = h$.

Note from Eqs. (6.15) and (6.16), that for $i^{'} \neq i$, $a_{ij} = a_{i'j}$ and $b_{ij} = b_{i'j}$ for $j \in \{r, h\}$. Hence, denote $a_r = a_{ir}$ and $b_r = b_{ir}$ for $i = 1, 2, .., N_r$; and denote $a_c = a_{ic}$ and $b_c = b_{ic}$ for $i = 1, 2, .., N_c$; and denote $a_h = a_{ih}$ and $b_h = b_{ih}$ for $i = 1, 2, .., N_h$.

In addition, the coefficients a_r, a_c, a_h, b_r, b_c, and b_h are computed from Eqs. (6.15) and (6.16) as:

$$a_r = \frac{\overline{\theta} - \mu + \eta\overline{\theta} + Nf_c\eta\overline{\theta}(m_c - 1) - Nf_h\eta\overline{\theta}(1 - m_h)}{\lambda(N+1)}, \tag{6.17}$$

$$a_c = \frac{\overline{\theta} - \mu + \eta\overline{\theta} + Nf_c\eta\overline{\theta}(m_c - 1) - Nf_h\eta\overline{\theta}(1 - m_h)}{\lambda(N+1)} - \frac{\eta\overline{\theta}(m_c - 1)}{\lambda}, \tag{6.18}$$

$$a_h = \frac{\overline{\theta} - \mu + \eta\overline{\theta} + Nf_c\eta\overline{\theta}(m_c - 1) - Nf_h\eta\overline{\theta}(1 - m_h)}{\lambda(N+1)} + \frac{\eta\overline{\theta}(1 - m_h)}{\lambda}, \tag{6.19}$$

$$b_r = \frac{\eta - Nf_c\eta(m_c - 1) - Nf_h\eta(m_h - 1)}{\lambda(N+1)}, \tag{6.20}$$

$$b_c = \frac{\eta - Nf_c\eta(m_c - 1) - Nf_h\eta(m_h - 1)}{\lambda(N+1)} + \frac{\eta(m_c - 1)}{\lambda}, \tag{6.21}$$

and

$$b_h = \frac{\eta - Nf_c\eta(m_c - 1) - Nf_h\eta(m_h - 1)}{\lambda(N+1)} + \frac{\eta(m_h - 1)}{\lambda}, \tag{6.22}$$

respectively.

Also, the asset price is computed from Eq. (6.6) as:

$$P = E\left(\theta \,|A + BS + x = D\right) = \overline{\theta} + \frac{B\sigma_\theta^2}{B^2\sigma_S^2 + \sigma_x^2}(D - A - B\overline{\theta}). \tag{6.23}$$

In addition, Eqs. (6.11) and (6.23) imply that

$$\mu = \overline{\theta}, \tag{6.24}$$

and

$$\lambda = \frac{B\sigma_\theta^2}{B^2\sigma_S^2 + \sigma_x^2}, \tag{6.25}$$

where $\sigma_S^2 = \sigma_\theta^2 + \sigma_\epsilon^2$.

Also, substituting Eqs. (6.20), (6.21), and (6.22) into the definition of B results in:

$$B = \frac{N}{\lambda}\left(f_c m_c - f_h - f_c + f_h m_h + 1\right). \tag{6.26}$$

In addition, substituting Eq. (6.26) into Eq. (6.25) gives rise to:

$$\lambda^2 = \left(\frac{N\eta\left(f_c(m_c - 1) + f_h(m_h - 1) + 1\right)}{N+1}\right)\frac{\sigma_\theta^2}{\sigma_x^2} - \left(\frac{N\eta\left(f_c(m_c - 1) + f_h(m_h - 1) + 1\right)}{N+1}\right)^2\frac{\sigma_S^2}{\sigma_x^2}. \tag{6.27}$$

Note from (6.27) that there is one positive and one negative solution for the parameter λ. Hence, the positive solution for λ is chosen to ensure that the second-order conditions of optimization problem (6.7) hold and the equilibrium price is an increasing function of the total demand for the asset.

Denote the equilibrium market orders for the asset of rational, conservatism, and heuristic traders as X_r, X_c and X_h, respectively. Using Eqs. (6.8) through (6.11), and Eqs. (6.17) through (6.25), the equilibrium market orders for the asset of rational, conservatism, and heuristic traders and the equilibrium asset price are computed as:

$$X_r = \frac{\eta(1 + Nf_c(1 - m_c) - Nf_h(m_h - 1))(S - \overline{\theta})}{\lambda(N+1)}, \tag{6.28}$$

$$X_c = \frac{\eta(1 + Nf_c(1 - m_c) - Nf_h(m_h - 1))(S - \overline{\theta})}{\lambda(N+1)} + \frac{(m_c - 1)\eta(S - \overline{\theta})}{\lambda}, \tag{6.29}$$

$$X_h = \frac{\eta(1 + Nf_c(1 - m_c) - Nf_h(m_h - 1))(S - \overline{\theta})}{\lambda(N+1)} + \frac{(m_h - 1)\eta(S - \overline{\theta})}{\lambda}, \tag{6.30}$$

and

$$P = \overline{\theta} + \frac{\eta(N + Nf_h(m_h - 1) - Nf_c(1 - m_c))(S - \overline{\theta})}{N + 1}, \tag{6.31}$$

respectively.

The terms $Nf_h(m_h - 1)$ and $Nf_c(1 - m_c)$ measure the total representativeness heuristic and the total conservatism bias in the market, respectively. They both affect the trading positions of rational, conservatism, and heuristic traders and the asset price (see Eqs. (6.28), (6.29), (6.30), and (6.31)).

6.3 The Results

This section presents detailed analysis on how the conservatism bias and representativeness heuristic cause the asset price to overreact or underreact to good news or bad news. Before the analysis, some definitions are first specified below:

In this model, the asset price overreaction to new information occurs if in response to the new information, rational traders buy (sell) the asset and at the same time, the asset price is higher (lower) than what it would in the market with only rational traders (i.e., $f_c = 0$ and $f_h = 0$); on the other hand, the asset price underreaction to new information occurs if in response to the new information, rational traders buy (sell) the asset and at the same time, the asset price is not as high (low) as it would be in the market with only rational traders (i.e., $f_c = 0$ and $f_h = 0$).

In addition, the asset price for the asset market with only rational traders (denoted as P_r) is computed from Eq. (6.31) as:

$$P_r = \overline{\theta} + \frac{N\eta(S - \overline{\theta})}{N + 1}. \tag{6.32}$$

Also, using Eq. (6.32), Eq. (6.31) is rewritten as:

$$P - P_r = \frac{\eta(Nf_h(m_h - 1) - Nf_c(1 - m_c))(S - \overline{\theta})}{N + 1}. \tag{6.33}$$

Hence, according to Eq. (6.33), if $Nf_h(m_h - 1) > Nf_c(1 - m_c)$, then, in response to the good news, $P > P_r$; and in response to the bad news, $P < P_r$. In addition, if the total representativeness heuristic is smaller than the total conservatism bias in the market, then, in response to the good news, $P < P_r$; and in response to bad news, $P > P_r$.

The following examines how the conservatism bias and representativeness heuristic cause the asset price to overreact or underreact to the good news.

Note from Eq. (6.28) that if the total representativeness heuristic minus the total conservatism bias in the market is less than one (i.e., $Nf_h(m_h-1)-Nf_c(1-m_c) < 1$), then rational traders buy the asset in response to the good news. Also, note from Eq. (6.33) that if the total representativeness heuristic is greater than the total conservatism bias in the market (i.e, $Nf_h(m_h-1)-Nf_c(1-m_c) > 0$), then $P > P_r$. Hence, if the total representativeness heuristic minus the total conservatism bias in the market is greater than zero but less than one (i.e., $0 < Nf_h(m_h - 1) - Nf_c(1 - m_c) < 1$), then, in response to the good news, rational traders buy the asset and at the same time, the asset price is higher than what it would be in the market with only rational traders. In other words, the asset price overreacts to the good news.

The alternative inequalities of $0 < Nf_h(m_h - 1) - Nf_c(1 - m_c) < 1$ consist of $Nf_h(m_h - 1) < Nf_c(1 - m_c)$ and $Nf_h(m_h - 1) - Nf_c(1 - m_c) > 1$. If $Nf_h(m_h - 1) < Nf_c(1 - m_c)$, then rational traders buy the asset in response to the good news and at the same time, $P < P_r$ (see Eqs. (6.28) and (6.33)). That is, the asset price underreacts to the good news. In addition, if $Nf_h(m_h - 1) - Nf_c(1 - m_c) > 1$, then rational traders sell the asset in response to the good news and at the same time, $P > P_r$ (see Eqs. (6.28) and (6.33)). That is, the asset price underreacts to the good news.

The above results are formally stated in Proposition 1 below:

Proposition 1 The asset price overreacts to good news if $0 < Nf_h(m_h - 1) - Nf_c(1 - m_c) < 1$; and the asset price underreacts to good news if $f_h(m_h - 1) - f_c(1 - m_c) < 0$ or $Nf_h(m_h - 1) - Nf_c(1 - m_c) > 1$.

The intuition for the results of Proposition 1 is as follows. Note that if the total representativeness heuristic minus the total conservatism bias in the market is less than one, then rational traders buy the asset in response to the good news. Also, note that if the total representativeness heuristic is greater than the total conservatism bias in the market, then in the presence of the good news, the impact on the asset price coming from heuristic traders dominates that coming from conservatism traders in the market. In addition, since a heuristic trader has a larger conditional mean of the asset payoff than a rational trader does in the case of the informational signal indicating good news (due to representativeness heuristic), it follows that the asset price is higher than what it would be in the market with only rational traders. Thus, if the total representativeness heuristic minus the total conservatism bias in the market is greater than zero but less than one, then asset price overreaction to the good news occurs.

On the other hand, if the total conservatism bias is greater than the total representativeness heuristic in the market, then in the presence of the good news, the impact on the asset price coming from conservatism traders dominates that coming from heuristic traders in the market. In addition, note that due to conservatism bias, a conservatism trader has a smaller conditional mean of the asset payoff than a rational trader does in the case of the informational signal indicating good news. Hence, the asset price is not as high as it would be in the market with only rational traders. That is, if the total conservatism bias is greater than the total representativeness heuristic in the market, then asset price underreaction to the good news occurs.

However, if the total representativeness heuristic minus the total conservatism bias in the market is greater than one, then in response to the good news, rational traders sell the asset and also, the impact on the asset price coming from heuristic traders dominates that coming from conservatism traders. In addition, note that a heuristic trader has a larger conditional mean of the asset payoff than a rational trader does in the case of the informational signal indicating good news. Hence, the asset price is not as low as it would be in the market with only rational traders. In other words, the asset price underreacts to the good news if the total representativeness heuristic minus the total conservatism bias in the market is greater than one.

The remaining section discusses how the conservatism bias and representativeness heuristic cause the asset price to overreact or underreact to bad news.

Note that if $Nf_h(m_h - 1) - Nf_c(1 - m_c) > 1$, then rational traders buy the asset in response to the bad news and at the same time, $P < P_r$ (see Eqs. (6.28) and (6.33)). That is, the asset price underreacts to the bad news if $Nf_h(m_h - 1) - Nf_c(1 - m_c) > 1$.

On the other hand, if $Nf_h(m_h - 1) - Nf_c(1 - m_c) < 1$, then rational traders sell the asset in response to the bad news (see Eq. (6.28)). In addition, if $f_h(m_h - 1) > f_c(1 - m_c)$, then $P < P_r$ (see Eq. (6.33)). Thus, the asset price overreacts to the bad news if $0 < Nf_h(m_h - 1) - Nf_c(1 - m_c) < 1$. Alternatively, if $f_h(m_h - 1) < f_c(1 - m_c)$ (naturally, $Nf_h(m_h - 1) - Nf_c(1 - m_c) < 1$), then $P > P_r$ (see Eq. (6.33)). Hence, the inequality of $P > P_r$, together with rational traders selling the asset in response to the bad news, implies that the asset price underreacts to the bad news.

The above results are formally presented in Proposition 2 below:

Proposition 2 The asset price overreacts to bad news if $0 < Nf_h(m_h - 1) - Nf_c(1 - m_c) < 1$; and the asset price underreacts to bad news if $Nf_h(m_h - 1) - Nf_c(1 - m_c) > 1$ or $f_h(m_h - 1) - f_c(1 - m_c) < 0$.

The reasons for the results of Proposition 2 are as follows. Note that if the total representativeness heuristic minus the total conservatism bias in the market is less than one, then rational traders sell the asset in response to the bad news. Also, note that if the total representativeness heuristic is greater than the total conservatism bias in the market, then the impact on the asset price coming from heuristic traders dominates that coming from conservatism traders in the market. In addition, since a heuristic trader has a smaller conditional mean of the asset payoff than a rational trader does in the case of the informational signal indicating bad news, it follows that the asset price is lower than what it would be in the market with only rational traders. Thus, the asset price overreaction to the bad news occurs if the total representativeness heuristic minus the total conservatism bias in the market is greater than zero but less than one.

In addition, if the total conservatism bias is greater than the total representativeness heuristic in the market, then in the presence of bad news, the impact on the asset price coming from conservatism traders dominates that coming from heuristic traders in the market. In addition, note that due to conservatism bias, a conservatism trader has a larger conditional mean of the asset payoff than a rational trader does in the case of the informational signal indicating bad news. Hence, the asset price is not as low as it would be in the market with only rational traders. Thus, if the total conservatism bias is greater than the total representativeness heuristic in the market, then the asset price underreacts to the bad news.

Also, if the total representativeness heuristic minus the total conservatism bias in the market is greater than one, then in response to the bad news, rational traders buy the asset and also, the impact on the asset price coming from heuristic traders dominates that coming from conservatism traders. In addition, since a heuristic trader has a smaller conditional mean of the asset payoff than a rational trader does in the case of the informational signal indicating bad news, it follows that the asset price is not as high as it would be in the market with only rational traders. In other words, the asset price underreacts to the bad news if the total representativeness heuristic minus the total conservatism bias in the market is greater than one.

6.4 Concluding Remarks

This chapter attempts to explain the phenomena of the asset price overreaction or underreaction to good news or bad news by using psychological biases, namely conservatism and representativeness. Specifically, this chapter constructs a static model of an asset market allowing for strategic interaction among traders. Due to the conservatism bias, conservatism traders are slow to update their beliefs about the asset payoff. In addition, due to the representativeness heuristic, heuristic traders place too much weight on current new information and not enough on their prior knowledge. Both conservatism traders and heuristic traders impact the asset price through their conditional mean of the asset payoff.

This chapter shows that whether the asset price overreacts or underreacts to the new information depends on the proportion of conservatism traders, the proportion of heuristic traders, the degree of conservatism bias, the degree of representativeness heuristic and the number of traders in the market. Specifically, the asset price overreacts to good news and bad news if the total representativeness heuristic minus the total conservatism bias in the market is greater than zero but less than one; otherwise, the asset price underreacts to good news and bad news.

Chapter 7
Conclusion

Empirical literature suggests that conservatism bias causes only asset price underreaction to new information and representativeness heuristic causes only asset price overreaction to new information. This book formally examines the role of conservatism bias and representativeness heuristic in determining asset price overreaction or underreaction to new information. Specifically, the models in Chaps. 2–5 of this book prove theoretically that either conservatism bias or representativeness heuristic is capable of generating both asset price overreaction and underreaction to new information. These results hold in a competitive securities market with noise traders or a security market with imperfect competition allowing strategic interaction among traders. Although the results in Chaps. 2–5 are purely theoretical, they shed some light on the cause of the asset price overreaction and underreaction to new information. The model in Chap. 6 attempts to build a realistic model to explain the cause of the asset price underreaction or overreaction to new information by using both conservatism bias and representativeness heuristic.

The future research direction in this area is to further explore how conservatism bias and representativeness heuristic can be used to explain the empirical phenomena of asset price overreaction or underreaction to new information.

G. Y. Luo, *Asset Price Response to New Information*, SpringerBriefs in Finance,
DOI 10.1007/978-1-4614-9369-3_7,

Appendix

Theorem 1: If two random variables X^* and Y^* obey a joint normal distribution, then $E\,(X^*\,|Y^* = Y) = E(X^*) + \frac{Cov(X^*,Y^*)}{Var(Y^*)}(Y - E(Y^*))$ and $Var\,(X^*\,|Y^* = Y) = Var(X^*) - \frac{[Cov(X^*,Y^*)]^2}{Var(Y^*)}$, where Y is the realization of Y^* (See Hoel 1962).

G. Y. Luo, *Asset Price Response to New Information,* SpringerBriefs in Finance,
DOI 10.1007/978-1-4614-9369-3,

Appendix

Theorem [illegible] and normal distribution. [illegible] and [illegible]

[illegible] where k is the [illegible] (see Hoel 1962).

[illegible]

References

Barberis, N., Shleifer, A., & Vishny, R. (1998). A model of investor sentiment. *Journal of Financial Economics, 49,* 307–343.
Bernard, V., & Thomas, J. (1989). Post-earnings-announcement drift: Delayed price response or risk premium? *Journal of Accounting Research, 27,* 1–33.
Daniel, K., Hirshleifer, D., & Subrahmanyam, A. (1998). Investor psychology and security market under- and overreactions. *Journal of Finance, 53,* 1839–1886.
De Bondt, W., & Thaler, R. (1985). Does the stock market overreact? *Journal of Finance, 40,* 793–808.
Desai, H., & Jain, P. (1997). Long-run common stock returns following splits and reverse splits. *Journal of Business, 70,* 409–433.
Douks, J., & McKnight, P. (2005). European momentum strategies, information diffusion and investor conservatism. *European Financial Management, 11*(3), 313–338.
Edwards, W. (1968). Conservatism in human information processing. In B. Kleimutz (Ed.), *Formal representation of human judgement* (pp. 17–52). New York: Wiley.
Fama, E. (1970). Efficient capital markets: A review of theory and empirical work. *Journal of Finance, 25,* 383–417.
Fischer, P., & Verrecchia, R. (1999). Public information and heuristic trade. *Journal of Accounting and Economics, 27*(1), 89–124.
Frazzini, A. (2006). The disposition effect and under-reaction to news. *Journal of Finance, 62,* 2017–2046.
Grether, D. (1980). Bayes' rule as a descriptive model: The representativeness heuristic. *Quarterly Journal of Economics, 95,* 537–557.
Grinblatt, M., & Han, B. (2005). Prospect theory, mental accounting and momentum. *Journal of Financial Economics, 78,* 311–339.
Grossman, S., & Stiglitz, J. (1980). On the impossibility of informationally efficient markets. *American Economic Review, 70*(3), 393–408.
Hirshleifer, D., Lim, S., & Teoh, S. (2011). Limited investor attention and stock market misreaction to accounting information. *Review of Asset Pricing Studies, 1*(1), 35–73.
Hoel, P. (1962). *Introduction to mathematical statistics* (p. 200). New York: Wiley.
Hong, H., & Stein, J. (1999). A unified theory of underreaction, momentum trading and overreaction in asset markets. *Journal of Finance, 54,* 2143–2184.
Ikenberry, D., Lakonishok, J., & Vermaelen, T. (1995). Market under-reaction to open market share repurchases. *Journal of Financial Economics, 39,* 181–208.
Ikenberry, D., Rankine, G., & Stice, E. (1996). What do stock splits really signal? *Journal of Financial and Quantitative Analysis, 31,* 357–377.
Jegadeesh, N., & Titman, S. (1993). Returns to buying winners and selling losers: Implications for stock market efficiency. *Journal of Finance, 48,* 65–91.
Jegadeesh, N., & Titman, S. (2001). Profitability of momentum strategies: An evaluation of alternative explanations. *Journal of Finance, 56*(2), 699–720.

G. Y. Luo, *Asset Price Response to New Information,* SpringerBriefs in Finance, DOI 10.1007/978-1-4614-9369-3,

Kahneman, D., & Tversky, A. (1973). On the psychology of prediction. *Psychological Review, 80,* 237–251.

Kyle, A. (1985). Continuous auctions and insider trading. *Econometrica, 53,* 1315–1335.

Lakonishok, J., & Vermaelen, T. (1990). Anomalous price behavior around repurchase tender offers. *Journal of Finance, 45,* 455–477.

Loughran, T., & Ritter, J. (1995). The new issues puzzle. *Journal of Finance, 50,* 23–51.

Luo, G. (2013). Can representativeness heuristic traders survive in a competitive security market? *Journal of Financial Markets, 16*(1), 152–164.

Michaely, R., Thaler, R., & Womack, K. (1995). Price reactions to dividend initiations and omissions. *Journal of Finance, 50,* 573–608.

Ritter, J. (1991). The long-term performance of initial public offerings. *Journal of Finance, 46,* 3–27.

Shefrin, H., & Statman, M. (1985). The disposition to sell winners too early and ride losers too long: Theory and evidence. *Journal of Finance, 40*(3), 777–790.

Spiess, D., & Affleck-Graves, J. (1995). Underperformance in long-run stock returns following seasoned equity offerings. *Journal of Financial Economics, 38,* 243–267.

Tversky, A., & Kahneman, D. (1974). Judgment under uncertainty: Heuristics and biases. *Science, 185,* 1124–1131.

MIX
Papier aus verantwortungsvollen Quellen
Paper from responsible sources
FSC® C105338

If you have any concerns about our products,
you can contact us on
ProductSafety@springernature.com

In case Publisher is established outside the EU,
the EU authorized representative is:
Springer Nature Customer Service Center GmbH
Europaplatz 3, 69115 Heidelberg, Germany

Printed by Libri Plureos GmbH
in Hamburg, Germany